Piper Cubs

Other Books in the Flying Classics Series

Piper Cubs

Peter M. Bowers

TAB **AERO**

Division of McGraw-Hill, Inc.

Blue Ridge Summit, PA 17294-0850

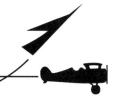

pbk 4 5 6 7 8 9 10 11 DOC/DOC 9 9 8 7 6 5

Library of Congress Cataloging -in-Publication Data

Bowers, Peter M.
    Piper Cubs /by Peter M. Bowers.
       p.   cm.
    Includes index.
    ISBN 0-8306-2170-9 (pbk.)
    1. Piper airplanes.   1. Title.
  TL686.P5B68 1992
  629.133'343--dc20   92-34049
                                            CIP

Acquisitions Editor: Jeff Worsinger
Editorial team: Charles Spence, Editor
           Susan Wahlman, Supervising Editor
           Joanne Slike, Executive Editor
           Joann Woy, Indexer
Production team: Katherine G. Brown, Director
           Susan E. Hansford, Typesetting
           Ollie Harmon, Typesetting
           Tine M. Sourbier, Typesetting
           Rose McFarland, Layout
           Kelly S. Christman, Proofreader
Design team: Jaclyn J. Boone, Designer
           Brian Allison, Associate Designer
Cover design: Holberg Design, York, Pa.   FCS
Cover illustration: Larry Selman, Waynesboro, Pa.   3997

Contents

Photographs and acknowledgments

I have collected most of the Taylor/Piper Cub photographs used in this book over a period of more than 50 years. Some, however, I sought out in the 1990–1991 period specifically to fill perceived gaps in Cub history and photo coverage. Unfortunately, not every Cub variant or experiment produced by the factory was photographed, not even the initial configuration of the very first Cub, so the photo coverage has unavoidable gaps.

Photo sources vary greatly. In addition to those taken by myself or obtained from other photo collectors, some prints have been obtained from the manufacturer, the U.S. Armed Forces, various Cub owners and operators, and museums and private archives.

Many of the photos are printed from original negatives in my files. When a negative or print has been obtained from another collector who was also the photographer, the published photo is credited to him. My apologies to those photographers who might find their photos miscredited. Old negatives and prints might pass through several hands over time, so determining the actual photographer or originating organization several decades after the fact is not always possible. Prints and negatives of unknown origin obtained from other collectors are credited to the collectors from whom they were obtained.

Pictures from known but no longer available sources obtained from other collectors, or a known photographer's photo obtained from another collector, split a credit line, as "Chalmers Johnson via Peter Berry."

The process of contacting others in the accumulation of Cub material turned up many contradictions in accepted Cub history that called for further research. Also, new and previously unknown facts and photos that I unearthed resulted in the reorganization of some of the manuscript and photo presentations in the book.

The following individuals were directly involved in the preparation of this book, and their assistance is greatly appreciated. Others, whose previously on-hand photos have been used, are acknowledged in the photo credit lines.

Alan Abel
Alaska Aviation Heritage Museum
John Amendola
Peter Berry
Bud Blancher
Robert Cavanagh
Golda Cox
Don "Bucky" Dawson
James Dilonardo
Don Downie
Fred Freeman
David Gauthier
Ernie Heald
Bud McHolland
Leo Kohn
Jack Krall
William Larkins
Howard Levy
David Lucabaugh
Mitch Mayborn
Robert Mikesh
David Menard
James Morrow
Gordon McNulty
Kenneth Molson
Dennis Parks

Ed Peck
Roger Peperell
Norm Petersen
Russell Phelinger
James Ruotsala
Bill Stratton
Clyde Smith, Sr.
Richard E. Smith
Kenneth Sumney
San Diego Aerospace Museum
Seattle Museum of Flight
Gordon Swanborough
Molt Taylor
Norman Taylor
Robert Taylor
Charles Trask
Russell Ulrich
John Underwood
U.S. Air Force Museum
U.S. Army Aviation Museum
Ray Wagner
Richard Wagner
Max Witters, Jr.

Introduction

Between them, the Taylor Aircraft Company and its successor, the Piper Aircraft Company, introduced 11 separately designated and certificated "Cub" models between 1930 and 1949. These planes ranged from two to four places and from 37 to 115 initial horsepower. The last of them, the PA-18 "Super Cub," started with 95 horsepower, but the major production version uses 150 hp while some post-delivery conversions use 180 hp. The Super Cub is still in production in 1992, establishing a remarkable production life of 62 years (so far, less a couple of short gaps) for what is essentially a single basic design.

However, mention the word "Cub" in the aeronautical sense among almost any group of people, aviation-oriented or otherwise, and the picture that comes to most minds is the little yellow putt-putt trainer or sport plane, not the hard-working jack-of-all-trades Super Cub or the nearly forgotten three- and four-place models.

Cubs are different things to different people, depending on the person's position in aviation. To old-timers who learned to fly in them, Cubs bring pleasant memories of a bygone era, when flying was more fun, being a pilot was something special, and the airspace was subjected to less regulation and control. Many present-day students and low-time licensed pilots who trained on modern all-metal "winged automobiles" with tricycle landing gear look down on the low-powered Cubs as obsolete "ragwings," in addition to being underpowered, slow, and, still worse, "treacherous taildraggers."

To some segments of busy commercial aviation, all low-powered models, Cubs and their kind, with their slow speed and lack of communication, are considered a hazard to others and should be ruled out of the sky. To everyone in the sport-aviation movement, both antique and homebuilt, the low-powered Cub, although an admitted anachronism in today's environment, is a treasured survivor of the past that still functions as a reliable and economical sportplane, not a museum piece. No modern entry-level airplane built since 1950 can approach the operating economy and easy maintenance of a J-3 Cub.

The late-model Super Cub, on the other hand, is an entirely different bird and shares only the basic construction and appearance of the low-powered model. It is a thoroughly modern airplane, with all the electrical and electronic gear needed to operate in modern high-density traffic. It performs such a wide variety of tasks in tight quarters that it has been dubbed "the poor man's helicopter." Small wonder that it has remained in production since 1949.

Altogether, Taylor and Piper built nearly 40,000 production airplanes that qualify for the name "Cub." These planes include military variants, like the L-4 and the HE-1, that are still basically Cubs. Of these, some 11,000 are still on the U.S. civil register.

Because of its numbers, the name "Cub" has become a generic term in aviation vocabulary. Low-powered Cubs have given their name to a whole class of airplane, not just Taylors and Pipers. To many people, any low-powered airplane is a Cub, and the small uncontrolled airports where no-radio lightplanes congregate have long been called "Cubvilles" because of the predominance of Cubs at those sites.

Perhaps no tribute to the Cub surpasses that given by the U.S. government. In 1991, the post office issued a 40-cent airmail stamp honoring the Cub's producer, identifying him as *William T. Piper, Aviation Pioneer*. In the background of the full-color portrait of Piper, which dominates the stamp, is a little yellow Cub.

This book describes each of the designated Cub models in sufficient detail to enable you to distinguish visually between such J-3 Cubs as the J-3C-40 and the J-3C-65, the prewar and postwar J-3C-65s, and the PA-18-125 and PA-18-135. Separate chapters describe some of the unique activities of the Cubs and the modifications that ingenious owners and operators have made to the basic tandem two-seater Cub to make it the world's most versatile airplane.

Through the years, aviation in the United States has come under the jurisdiction of different government agencies, the most recent being the Federal Aviation Administration (FAA) of the Department of Transportation. Many regulations affecting the Cub, as with other aircraft of that era, came from predecessor offices. However, for simplicity of readership, I refer to any federal aviation agency as "FAA," the currently familiar name.

1

The Taylor Brothers' enterprises

As with many small airplane manufacturing organizations of the 1920s, the Taylor Brothers Aircraft Corporation of Rochester, New York, evolved out of aircraft maintenance and repair activities. Two brothers, Clarence Gilbert ("C.G.") and Gordon A. Taylor, assisted their father in the operation of the North Star Aerial Service Corporation in Rochester. As an extra project beyond their routine business, the Taylors rebuilt a war-surplus Curtiss JN–4D "Jenny" and made enough modifications so that it was more than just another Jenny—it was, in their minds at least, their own creation.

Original airplane designs

In 1925 the Taylors created an entirely original design, a three-seat monoplane with the pilot in an open cockpit and two passengers in an enclosed cabin. In the absence of any suitable American engine other than the 90-hp war-surplus Curtiss OX–5, the engine they chose was a 110-hp French Anzani 10-cylinder air-cooled radial. This configuration was relatively daring for the time, with cabin monoplanes and radial engines rarities in 1925.

In those days, it was possible for a clever person with only a high-school education to design a complete airplane. There were no government requirements for stress or aerodynamic calculations for approval of the design. There were neither design approval nor licensing requirements for American aircraft in 1925. Engineering could be and often was a largely empirical procedure—the sizes of spars, longerons, etc., were determined by inspecting successful equivalent designs, and as long as one stayed within the well-established proportions that were the industry standard, an acceptable airplane would result. Unfortunately, no photos are known to exist of this first original Taylor design, which was registered 2594 after registration of U.S. aircraft became mandatory in 1927.

Success of the monoplane encouraged the brothers to go into the airplane manufacturing business. The Taylor Brothers Aircraft Manufacturing Company was formed at Rochester in August 1927, and by September construction of a new personal monoplane with side-by-side seating for two was underway. It was completed in February 1928. The engine was another Anzani, a 90-hp model.

The new design (Fig. 1-1) was advertised as the "Arrow Wing Chummy," Model A–2; A for the first model of the new company, –2 for two seats. With registrations and licensing now in effect, the A–2 received an experimental license and registration X-4203. Because a serial number was also required (referred to as Constructor's Number, or C/N, by aviation historians and throughout this book), it was given C/N 3. This C/N acknowledged the rebuilt Jenny as the first Taylor airplane and the 1925 monoplane (which did not have a C/N when registered) as the second.

In April 1928, the company was renamed the Taylor Brothers Aircraft Corporation, and the next airplane, a refined A–2 with another imported engine, the 84-hp Ryan-Siemens, appeared. The engine was the German

1-1 The first airplane built by the Taylor Brothers Aircraft Manufacturing Company in 1927 was the Arrow Wing Chummy, Model A-2, C/N 3. It featured a French Anzani radial engine and side-by-side seating for two.

Siemens-Halske SH–11, imported by T. Claude Ryan and marketed as the Ryan-Siemans 7 (for 7 cylinders). Registered X-4901 with C/N 4, the second A–2 was marketed as the Taylor A–2 instead of the Arrow Wing. It was displayed at the Detroit Air Show in April 1928 (Fig. 1-2), but crashed soon afterward, killing Gordon Taylor.

The ill-fated Taylor A–2 was followed by two unnumbered designs identified simply as Taylor Specials, C/Ns 5 and 6. It is believed that C/N 6 was never completed.

1-2 The second A-2 Chummy, C/N 4, showed great refinement over the first, and used a German Ryan-Siemens engine, shown here at the 1928 Detroit Aviation show shortly before its fatal crash.

While the A–2 model showed promise, it had room for improvement, especially in the powerplant department. New American air-cooled radials were now available in the desired horsepower range, so the improved Chummy was offered as the Model B–2 (Fig. 1-3) with a 90-hp Kinner K–5 (for 5 cylinders). C/Ns 7 and 8 were unlicensed, only registered, but C/N 9, while it did not quality for a full Approved Type Certificate (ATC), did receive the lesser Category-2, or Memo, certificate 2-114 on August 27, 1929. C/Ns 12 and 14 were also approved. These approvals testified to C.G. Taylor's increased skill as an engineer, because the stress and performance calculations required for even a Category-2 approval were considerable.

Move to Pennsylvania

Considering his manufacturing facility in Rochester inadequate, C.G. Taylor sought a new location for the Taylor Brothers Aircraft Corporation. At the

Edward Peck

1-3 Only three B-3 Chummys with 90-hp American Kinner engines received Approved Type Certificates and commercial licenses. This one is NC992V, C/N 14.

same time, the town of Bradford, Pennsylvania, was seeking new businesses to boost the local economy. For many years the country around Bradford had been a major oil-producing area, but the oil was nearly gone. As an incentive for Taylor Aircraft to move to Bradford, a citizen's committee offered a $50,000 purchase of Taylor stock and the use of a small ironworks bordering the local airport. Taylor accepted the offer and moved his operation to Bradford.

Enter William T. Piper

Bill Piper, a Harvard-educated veteran of the Spanish-American War, was a partner with Ralph Lloyd in an oil-recovery business called the Dallas Oil Company when the campaign to bring Taylor to town was underway. One of the promoters of the move had offices in the same building as Piper and his partner. The promoter dropped by and talked Lloyd into taking $400 worth of Taylor stock and an equal amount for Piper, who was out of the office. Piper then found that he had gotten into the airplane business without even knowing about it.

Soon afterward, the president of the Bradford Chamber of Commerce, Piper's old commanding officer, informed Piper that he wanted him on Taylor Aircraft's board of directors.

Production and bankruptcy

Taylor resumed production of the B–2 Chummy at Bradford, but, at a price of over $4000, it was not selling. In hope of winning some of the $150,000 prize money offered by the Daniel Guggenheim Fund for the development of a safe airplane, Taylor modified the second Rochester-built B-2, C/N 7, into the C-2. Its main new feature was a variable-incidence wing (Fig. 1-4). The plane was flown to New York City for the fly-off contest in December 1929, but it was rejected.

Prior to that time, Piper had done some research into the airplane marketing business and decided that what the company needed was a low-cost, bare-minimum training plane. C.G. Taylor agreed and started work on the new design.

1-4 The first B-2 Chummy, redesignated C-2, was modified for the 1929 Guggenheim Safe Airplane Competition.

The new factory produced the last three of the eight Chummies built and was rapidly going broke because the planes didn't sell in that early Depression year of 1930. That year saw the closure of many well-established aircraft factories with popular product lines. Taylor even built a primary glider (Fig. 1-5) in an attempt to break into the new and prospering glider market but without success. By this time, Piper was putting some of his own money into the plant to keep it open, and appointed himself treasurer.

Even so, the firm went bankrupt. Piper was the only bidder for the assets at the bankruptcy sale, and he acquired them for $761. Now the owner, he reorganized the firm as the Taylor Aircraft Company. Piper gave Taylor half-interest and the presidency and appointed him chief engineer, but retained control of the purse strings himself.

1-5 The last design of the Taylor Brothers Aircraft Corporation was the single Model D primary glider of 1930. It was a notable improvement over contemporary primaries in that it featured a welded-steel tube fuselage.

2

The Taylor Cubs
1930–1937

Before the bankruptcy and inspired by a demonstration of the new ultralight Aeronca C-2 with its 30-hp Aeronca engine, Taylor and Piper agreed that their future depended on building a good, low-powered, two-seat trainer. It proved to be one of the few things that those two disparate personalities ever agreed on in their 7-year association.

Designing an airplane was one thing; tailoring it to a specific market was another. Piper had strong feelings in the matter; he didn't want to sell to the private owner, he wanted to sell to flight instructors. He reasoned that by lowering the cost of flying lessons, more people could learn to fly. The current trainers in use were two- and three-seat biplanes of 90 hp and up, and lessons cost about $30 per hour. Piper believed that a simple low-powered trainer should reduce that cost by three-quarters, and it did.

Birth of the Taylor Cub

Taylor promptly went to work on a little tandem-seat design that used a wood-frame wing with built-up metal ribs, very similar in size to that of the Taylor primary glider. The airfoil was the well-established USA-35B. This airfoil would remain in use on all Taylor and Piper designs through the twin-engine PA-23 "Apache" introduced in 1958, and the PA-25 "Pawnee" duster/sprayer of 1959. Super Cubs retained the USA-35B.

The fuselage was welded-steel tubing, as was the tail. The wing was above the fuselage in the parasol position, but was so close to it that the occupants of the open cockpit could not get into the cockpit by the normal procedure of climbing over the side.

This dilemma produced an inspired piece of design work that was to be a standard feature of all the tandem-seat Taylor and Piper Cub models to follow. A long single door was installed on the right side of the fuselage to span both seats, but instead of being hinged at the front, it was hinged at the bottom and opened downward. A windshield fit between the wing and the forward fuselage, and the airfoil-shaped gravity fuel tank was on top of the fuselage above the front seat.

The choice of powerplant was a problem. No small engines were in production in America; even Aeronca was making its own 30-hp two-cylinder powerplant. Finally, an available engine appeared—a little two-cylinder air-cooled 20-hp model known as the Brownback "Tiger Kitten." Since a tiger kitten was a cub, Taylor's accountant, Gilbert Hadrel, was inspired to name the little airplane "The Cub," certainly one of the most appropriate names ever given to an airplane, and destined to become one of the most famous.

The Cub, designated E-2 in continuing Taylor letter designations (the glider was Model D), with the -2 indicating two seats, was ready to fly in September 1930. It was given constructor's number (C/N) 11 in a continuation of the previous Taylor C/Ns dating back to 1925. The first Cub was never licensed, even as an experimental model. It was merely "identified" by the registration number 10547.

The engine had been brought to the plant in an airplane by George Kirkendall, of Brownback Motors. It was a two-cylinder inverted air-cooled in-line with 77 cubic-inch displacement and delivered 20 hp at 2300 rpm. Unfortunately, no photos are known to exist showing it installed in the prototype Taylor Cub.

After the Brownback engine was installed, Kirkendall was allowed to make the first flight of the Cub. The Kitten just wasn't adequate, and the best that could be accomplished was a short straight-ahead trip down the runway with a little daylight showing under the wheels. The engine was removed and Kirkendall took it back to the factory.

Years later Kirkendall falsely claimed that he had told Taylor what kind of plane to design, that he was co-designer of the Cub, and that he had given it its name. These claims caused Taylor, in January 1983, to publish and distribute a statement refuting all of Kirkendall's claims and stating that he, C.G. Taylor, was the one and only designer of the Taylor Cub airplane.

In October, a better engine was tried, an imported 40-hp French Salmson AD-9, a neat little 9-cylinder radial (Fig. 2-1). This gave the Cub good performance, but was totally unsuitable for a small and economical American airplane. Not only was it foreign and built on metric tooling, it was expensive.

2-1 The first Cub, Taylor Model E-2, became a successful airplane after the original Brownback Tiger Kitten engine was replaced with the 40-hp French Salmson shown. Note the fuel tank in the center section of the wing and the vane-type airspeed indicator on the right jury strut. Designer C.G. Taylor is on the left, with test pilot Rensselaer C. "Bud" Havens.

The final engine tried in a second Cub in February 1931, was the brand-new, single-ignition 37-hp Continental A-40 built by Continental Motors of Detroit, Michigan. This little 4-cylinder air-cooled model, with each opposing bank of two cylinders cast as a single unit, had a displacement of 115 cubic inches and delivered 37 hp at 2800 rpm. This was the engine chosen for the production Taylor E-2 Cub.

Taylor grows

After the E-2 got into production, Taylor Aircraft became the leading producer of airplanes in its weight/power/price market. However, the early A-40 engine had teething problems. Taylor bore the brunt of most of the problems, which led to a search for alternative powerplants and resulted in new model numbers for the Cub.

C.G. Taylor was having health problems in 1935, and spent much time away from the plant. Prior to one of his absences, Taylor asked a young engineer, Walter C. Jamouneau, to make some improvements to the E-2 short of structural changes. Jamouneau, encouraged by Piper, exceeded his mandate considerably, however, and converted the boxy E-2 into a plane with nicely curved tail surfaces and wingtips and a bona-fide cabin, the Model J-2.

When Taylor saw this, he was furious and fired all three of the engineering staff. A subsequent showdown with Piper resulted in a situation where one partner could settle the dispute by buying out the other. It ended with Piper buying Taylor's half of the company; W.T. Piper was now President as well as chairman of the board and treasurer. The fired engineers were re-hired, and Jamouneau became Chief Engineer at the age of 24.

The firm was prospering when disaster struck on the night of March 16/17, 1937. The Bradford plant burned down. Some complete airplanes were salvaged, plus enough material to continue production of the current J-2 model on a small scale. Search for a new factory resulted in a move to a former silk mill adjacent to the airport in Lock Haven, Pennsylvania. This move was instigated by Jacob W. (Jake) Miller, a Lock Haven flight operator and the local distributor of Taylor Cubs. He got Piper and the city fathers together. Piper refinanced the company, and production of the J-2 Cub was continued in Lock Haven in May 1937.

Business soon boomed again. With further financing through stock sales and the absence of Taylor—who had founded a competing firm, Taylorcraft—the company name was changed to Piper Aircraft Corporation in November 1937.

The Taylor Cub series

Taylor built only two Cub models in quantity, the original E-2 and the final model produced under the Taylor name, the J-2.

E-2. The second Cub built, C/N 12, registered 10594 and powered with the Continental A-40 (Fig. 2-2), did not win a full Approved Type Certificate (ATC) right away. It received the lower Category 2, or "Memo" certificate 2-358 on June 15, 1931, meaning that the airplane could carry the NC prefix letters to the registration number and be used commercially with certain limitations. The following 13 E-2 Cubs were built under 2-358. The full ATC A-455 was awarded on November 7, 1931, and covered C/Ns 26 and on.

The production E-2 was essentially like the prototype with minor improvements. The 9-gallon fuel tank was now in the fuselage, between the instrument panel and the firewall. One very significant improvement, and one to be retained by all future Cub models, was longitudinal trim by means of a jack screw operated by cable from the cockpit, that moved the leading edge of the horizontal stabilizer up and down. A later change was a removable engine mount for the radially-mounted A-40 engine, starting with C/Ns 66, 72, and up.

However, the E-2 was still an open-cockpit design. To increase passenger comfort in cold weather, Taylor devised transparent side panels for the cockpit, with a hinge-up panel on the right side mating with the hinge-down door (Fig. 2-3). This soon became a standard built-in feature.

2-2 The second Cub, Taylor serial number 12, was built to production standards. Note revised jury struts, deletion of fuel tank in center section, addition of adjustable horizontal stabilizer, and cut-out at rear of wing. The plane was not licensed when this photo was taken; the letters NC were scratched onto the photo negative later.

2-3 To protect occupants from the elements, Taylor offered optional removable side window panels for the E-2. This particular E-2 has been downgraded from a full standard license to "identified" status. Notice that the NC prefix of a licensed airplane has been painted out.

Continental worked hard to correct the troubles with the original A-40 engines and improved -2 and -3 models were used in later E-2s and retrofitted to earlier ones. The final A-40 used in the E-2 was the -4, which produced 40 hp at 2575 rpm but still had single ignition.

One flight requirement of the E-2 was that it be flown solo from the rear seat only. This seating was a balance problem inherited from most of the 2–3 seat open-cockpit biplanes built to that time. The pilot in the rear cockpit balanced the engine up front; the front seat was right on the center of gravity (CG) where the presence or absence of a passenger would not affect the longitudinal balance of the airplane. The allowed CG travel for the E-2 was only 4.5 inches.

Counting the unlicensed prototype, 353 E-2 Cubs were built to the end of production in February 1936. Standard coloring was silver with dark red or maroon trim. Gross weight was 925 pounds initially, increased to 970 pounds by 1935. Cost in 1932 was $1325, increased to $1475 in 1935.

F-2. Chronic troubles with the early A-40 engines led to a search for other suitable powerplants. First choice was the Aeromarine AR-340, a three-cylinder air-cooled radial. This had 160 cubic inch displacement and produced 40 hp at 2050 rpm (Fig. 2-4). Under prevailing FAA policy, a different engine in the same airframe required a new airplane model designation and a new ATC. The Aeromarine-powered Cub was given the next letter, F, and became the F-2. ATC A-525 was awarded on February 16, 1934 for C/Ns 40, 66, 74, and up. Gross weight was from 981 to 988 pounds with six pounds of baggage. The initial price was $1495.

Robert Esposito

2-4 Because the early Continental A-40 engines were troublesome, Taylor found a substitute in the three-cylinder 40 hp Aeromarine AR-340 radial engine. The rough-running radial was not popular.

The F-2 was not popular, and relatively few—approximately 33—were built. The F-2s are counted in the E-2 production total. Production of the F-2 ended with the Bradford fire.

Some E-2 owners changed their A-40 engines to AR-340s, but later, because of its own unsatisfactory characteristics, some owners of F-2s replaced the AR-340s with the improved A-40-4.

G-2. In a further search for a replacement for the A-40, Taylor went to the extreme of designing and building his own 35–40-hp engine. This was fitted to Cub C/N 149, registration X14756, which was then designated G-2. The one-only engine wasn't even mentioned in the technical publications of the day, and no details are known. The G-2 airplane soon got another engine and became the H-2.

H-2. The G-2 Cub was re-engined with a 35 hp Szekely SB-3-35, another 3-cylinder radial (Fig. 2-5). Displacement was 190 cubic inches and power was 35 hp at 1750 rpm. ATC A-572 was awarded on May 28, 1935, but no H-2 airplanes were built as such. The Szekely name has been widely mispronounced, usually as Zee-Klee or Zay-Kay. The name is Hungarian and is pronounced Say-Kai, according to the designer's nephew. The prototype, C/N 1419, had been the G-2 converted from an E-2 airframe, and the three other known H-2s, C/N 40, 66, and 74, were F-2 conversions. Gross weight was 981 pounds for ATC A-572, and no price figures are available.

2-5 A restored Taylor H-2 Cub with Szekely engine being run up at a 1992 fly-in.

The Szekely engine turned out to be an undesirable powerplant. The cast-iron cylinders frequently cracked around the mounting flanges and separated from the rest of the engine. The FAA required the installation of tie-rods or cables circling the engine at the cylinder heads to hold broken cylinders in place until the pilot could land.

J-2. As mentioned, Walter Jamouneau reworked an E-2, C/N 500, NX15951, into a new model, the J-2. In later years, this J designation came to be accepted as J-for-Jamouneau. Actually, it was logical progression from the

The Taylor Cubs   **13**

H-2, skipping the letter I that could be mistaken for the figure 1. Certainly no young engineer would have the audacity to name a new company model for himself.

Jamouneau's changes were considerably more than rounding off the square corners of the E-2 that Taylor had envisioned (Fig. 2-6). Besides the rounded wingtips and new tail shape, the J-2 had a refined nose for better engine cooling and a wider-track landing gear with a revised shock cord and tension strut arrangement. The rear turtledeck structure was raised to fair the fuselage into the wing and create a closed cabin with a three-piece windshield. However, the left side window frames were removable. Solo flight was still from the rear seat. The J-2 was initially advertised as "The New Cub."

Gordon S. Williams

2-6 Walter Jamouneau's re-design of the angular Taylor E-3 in late 1935 resulted in a new model number—J-2. Note the rounded wingtips, double-curved vertical tail surfaces, and more substantial cabin window framing. Note also that the unbalanced ailerons are hinged along the upper surface.

With the J-2 the tandem-seat Cub reached its final configuration. Subsequent models incorporated only minor detail changes.

The J-2 prototype was converted from an E-2, X15951, in October 1935, but started a new C/N series at 500. ATC A-595 was awarded February 14, 1936. The engine was still the single-cylinder A-40-2, -3, or -4, but some used the twin-ignition A-40-5. The J-2 did not get subsequent power increases. The FAA ruled that the SAE 1025 steel tubing in the fuselage was not strong enough for increased power or weight. However, some J-2s in several other countries are known to have become licensed with 65 hp Continental A-65 engines.

Gross weight was 930 pounds for C/Ns 500/599 and 1000 pounds for C/N 600 and up, with a 20-pound baggage allowance. Initial price was $1470, but increased production rates brought this down to $1270.

An aeronautical oddity approved for the J-2 was the Everel one-bladed propeller that supposedly got greater efficiency by not having two blades operating in each other's wake (Fig. 2-7).

2-7 A novelty offered as an option on the J-2 Cub and the later J-3 was the Everel one-bladed propeller. Efficiency was supposedly increased by having the single blade work in air undisturbed by another blade. The off-center thrust was hard on the engine's thrust bearings, so the Everel propeller was not around for long.

J-2S. Any J-2 fitted with floats (Fig. 2-8) had S-for-seaplane added to the model designation. There was no letter added for ski installations.

J-2X. Unofficial designation for one J-2, NX19518, C/N 1718, used as a test bed for the experimental 60-hp Glenn D. Angle 5-60 radial engine in 1938 (Fig. 2-9).

On March 24, 1937, shortly before the end of J-2 production, one or more J-2s were licensed under Memo Certificate 2-533. No information is available concerning the changes that resulted in this downgrade of the J-2.

The Western J-2 Cub

To meet increasing demand for the J-2 in the western U.S., an arrangement was made in 1936 whereby Aircraft Associates of Long Beach, California, would assemble J-2s from components built in Lock Haven. The Long Beach J-2s were given the name "Western Cub" (Fig. 2-10), but oddly, they were given a new ATC, A-620, issued December 23, 1936.

Gordon S. Williams

2-8 The J-2 was the first Cub licensed as a seaplane. When operated on floats, the J-2 and later Piper models added the letter S-for-Seaplane to the model designation, as J-2S. When put back on wheels, the S was dropped.

Warren Shipp via Ken Sumney

2-9 No J-2s were built with other than the 37–40-hp Continental A-40 engine. The designation J-2X was given to this example, modified in 1938 to serve as a flying test bed for the experimental Glenn D. Angle 5-60 radial engine, which was not put into production.

As a further oddity, the ATC did not spell out the specifications, serial numbers, or limitations in the usual way. It merely referred to ATC A-595 while stating that all major components must be manufactured by Taylor in Bradford. Wing spars and minor structural parts could be fabricated by Aircraft Associates.

The existence of the Aircraft Associates J-2 program was a boon to Taylor after the Bradford fire. Bradford continued to ship some components, but Aircraft Associates helped by building new fuselages and shipping them to Bradford.

Oliver R. Phillips

2-10 Not all of the J-2 Cubs were built by Taylor and Piper. At least 22 were built by Aircraft Associates in Long Beach, California, using some parts built by Taylor in Bradford, Pennsylvania. Note the different logo on the fin and that this example, photographed in April 1940, has had the engine exhaust system modified to accommodate a carburetor air heater.

Although the Western Cubs carried Bradford plant C/Ns, 22 C/Ns, those from 899/902, and 1245/1262, are listed for J-2s built, not merely assembled, at Long Beach. Western Cubs could be distinguished from Bradford Cubs by a notably different trademark on the fin, and by their known registration numbers: NC17233/17236, NC17810/17827. Assembly of the Western Cub ended after Taylor moved to Lock Haven.

Foreign J-2 assembly

In 1936 Taylor formed a subsidiary, Cub Aircraft Corporation, to assemble J-2s (and later J-3s) in other countries. A Canadian branch was established at Hamilton, Ontario, in 1937 and another in Copenhagen, Denmark, in 1938. Hamilton assembled 23 J-2s and the Danish plant assembled 15.

J-2 transition and finale

Altogether, 1207 J-2s were built to May 1938, but only 1140 were built as Taylor J-2s. Aside from the 22 Western Cubs, the new Piper Aircraft Company that succeeded Taylor Aircraft completed the final 67 J-2s. Many of these were exported, or assembled in Canada, and never received U.S. registration. The U.S. registered Piper J-2s are all in the following block of 39 U.S. registrations: NC20137/20175, plus 21408 and 21423.

3

The Piper J-3 Cub
1937–1942

Of the 11 certificated Cub models, the J-3 is by far the most famous. It was designed in 1937 and was produced continuously until early 1942. That period of development and production is covered in this chapter. Postwar J-3 production from 1945 to the final J-3 of 1947 is covered in chapter 6. Other Cub models of 1937–1942 are detailed in chapter 4.

The new Piper Aircraft Corporation, now situated in Lock Haven, Pennsylvania, continued production of the J-2 through 1937 and into early 1938. Some of the 1937 production was under the old Taylor name, but after the name change they became Pipers. Approximately the last 67 of the 1207 J-2s built were Piper J-2s.

Piper developed three new models from late 1937 to 1940, and quickly became the dominant manufacturer of light airplanes. In 1938 the company built 737 J-2 and J-3 Cubs. In 1939 it built 1806, including a new model, and rolled out 3016 in 1940. The government's civilian pilot training program (CPTP) adopted for colleges in 1939, created a huge new market for J-3s. Production continued to increase to where the 10,000th Cub was delivered before the end of 1941.

It is interesting to note that the CPTP program specified tandem seating for the training planes. Piper had the only tandem-seat lightplane suitable for the program at the time, and profited accordingly. Aeronca and Taylorcraft quickly produced tandem-seat variants of their standard side-by-side models. They did make CPTP sales but could not catch up with the

J-3s lead. Nearly three-quarters of the thousands of CPTP primary trainers were J-3 Cubs.

Civil airplane production in the U.S. ended early in 1942 and Piper became involved in war work. In addition to producing militarized versions of the J-3 and J-5 Cub models the company built non-aircraft products for the war effort.

Enter the J-3

Late in 1937 William Piper, Sr. put Jamouneau to work on an improved version of the J-2, using a J-2 with C/N 1800 as the prototype. Although the changes were nearly as extensive as those from the E-2 to the J-2, the new model did not get a new letter designation. Keeping the J-for-Jamouneau, the new Cub was designated J-3. The J-3 turned out to be exactly the right airplane at the right time, and quickly dominated the lightplane market.

The J-3, initially called the "Cub Sport" by Piper, retained the single-ignition Continental A-40 engine, nine-gallon fuel tank, three-piece windshield, spring-leaf tailskid, and brakeless wheels of the J-2, but featured many refinements. A new vertical tail shape with balanced rudder was adopted. The vertical fin was removable as on the J-2, but not when it was covered. Fabric from the top of the rear fuselage was carried up onto the fin during covering to make a neat fabric fillet between fuselage and fin, a detail previously seen on Stinson Reliants and some racing planes. This feature was retained for all subsequent Cub models.

Bucket seats instead of flat boards greatly increased cabin comfort. The ignition switch was moved from under the front seat to the left cabin wall above the window. The J-2 engine cowling was retained as was the split right-side door (Fig. 3-1).

There was also a marking change. The over-all color of the J-3 was the same "Cub yellow" as the late J-2s, but the triple fuselage stripe was replaced by a single tapered stripe that started aft of the firewall. Later, this was converted to a zigzag lightning streak. The color and streak remained standard for all but a few special J-3s to the end of post–WWII J-3 production.

The most significant change, and one that allowed great growth in the J-3 and subsequent Cubs, was the use of SAE X-4130 steel tubing for the fuselage. Its greater strength allowed the installation of higher power engines that had been denied the J-2.

Competitive improvements

Considering Piper's improved manufacturing facility, production of the initial Cub Sport model reached an approximate total of only 300. Improved models that outside circumstances forced on Piper quickly replaced the Cub Sport.

3-1 An early J-3 Cub Sport built under ATC A-660. Note similarity of nose and A-40 engine with short curved exhaust stacks to J-2. Some Cub Sports had spring-leaf tailskids; this one has a steerable tail wheel.

The first change was brakes and a steerable tail wheel. Aeronca had them on the side-by-side K model, which put the Cub at a disadvantage on the increasing number of airports having paved ramps, taxiways, and runways. For a first try, Tony Piper, one of William Piper's three sons, developed an adaptation of a bicycle coaster brake for the tail wheel, operated by a cable from the cockpit. This brake was only marginally successful, so the J-3 got new 8.00×4 wheels with hydraulic brakes operated by foot pedals in the cockpit. The separate actuators were for the rear seat pilot. Front pedals were connected by pull wires to the rear seat actuators. The arrangement worked fine.

The other forced changes were increases in power and even changes of powerplant. Continental now had competition from several other manufacturers of small engines that Piper's competition was eager to use. Continental's initial response was to convert the A-40 to twin ignition with the A-40-5, which enabled it to deliver an honest 40 hp. Unfortunately, the old engine didn't take the added power too well, so Continental came out with a new engine, the 50 hp A-50.

The new X-4130 fuselage allowed increased power with no other airframe modifications other than new cowls and mounts suited to the particular engines. Based on an FAA formula for required fuel vs. engine power, later Cubs adopted 12-gallon fuel tanks.

Continental's new A-50 engine had 171 cubic inch displacement, and the

50-hp Lycoming O-145 had 145. Like the original A-40, these engines were all four-cylinder, air-cooled flat, or "opposed" types. All started with single ignition but were forced by new regulations to adopt twin ignition. The 50-hp LM-3 which was the old Aeromarine AR-3 radial engine, had 160 cubic inches. There was also a 50-hp Menasco M-50, another flat four with 144 cubic inches. However, the M-50 retained single ignition which was eliminated for new designs under new engineering rules effective in 1938. The single ignition could continue in use on designs certificated prior to the new rules, but because neither Taylor nor Piper had used one before, it could not be used in the new Cubs.

After the new engines appeared, the engine manufacturers engaged in a power race. Increases came mainly from improving the metallurgy and lubrication, raising the compression ratio, and turning smaller diameter propellers at higher speed.

These powerplant and corresponding weight changes resulted in several additional ATCs being issued to J-3 Cubs powered with the different engines.

Other improvements

Some changes were simply product improvements worked out by Piper for improved manufacturing methods or better airplane flight characteristics. Others were safety-related items like carburetor air heaters and passenger-comfort items like cabin heating.

One very significant change was to replace the unbalanced plain-hinged ailerons (Fig. 3-2) with aerodynamically-balanced Frieze type (Fig. 3-3). This

3-2 This view of a deluxe J-3L Cub with Lycoming engine emphasizes the use of top-hinged plain ailerons on early Cub Sports. Note the wheel pants and running lights.

3-3 This J-3F-65 shows the Frieze ailerons that soon became production standard. Note that the three hinge points are set well back from the leading edge of the aileron.

type of aileron puts the leading edge below the wing surface when the aileron is moved to the UP position. This adds drag to the inside of the turn and reduces the amount of rudder movement needed to overcome the phenomenon known as adverse yaw.

Plain ailerons were used on early J-3s built under all five J-3 ATCs. Frieze ailerons became production items for all Cubs by early 1940 and could be retrofitted to earlier J-3s.

Another Piper-initiated addition was an engine starter. It consisted of a long rubber cord in the rear of the fuselage that the pilot wound up 35 turns with a hand crank. The cord was connected to the engine and turned it over when the pilot pulled the engage handle. This process was hardly worth the effort involved on the J-3 and was abandoned for that model, but it did see limited use on some later Piper models.

One major structural change came too late in 1941 to be widely used before J-3 production ended in 1942. This replaced the solid-wood wing spars with new extruded aluminum spars. These became standard for postwar J-3s.

The Piper J-3 Cub series—1937–1942

Under prevailing FAA policy, a change of engine in a certificated airplane required testing of that airplane/engine combination and the issuance of a new

ATC. A good example is the change from Taylor E-2 to F-2 and H-2 when using new engines. The J-3 departed from this procedure. It remained a J-3 regardless of engines, and identified the particular engine by a suffix letter—J-3C for Continental, J-3L for Lycoming, etc. Further dash numbers identified the power of the engine, as J-3C-50, J-3C-65, etc.

Production of the civil J-3 ended in February 1942 but military versions were built as O-58 and L-4 until 1945. (See Chapter 5.) Civil production resumed in September 1945, and finally ended in March 1947. In spite of new C/N series adopted for 1938 and later Piper models, the postwar J-3s continued the original C/N numbering dating back to the Taylor Brothers. A total of 6143 J-3 Cubs was built from 1937 to the end of civil production in 1942.

J-3 Sport. The J-3 Sport received ATC A-660 in November 1937. No letter was used to identify the 37-hp single-ignition Continental engine, Models A-40-2, -3, or -4. The prototype was given C/N 1800 out of the J-2 series, and the registration NX20000. This did not start a new run of registration numbers for the J-3; C/N 1801 through 1975, with a few gaps, continued registrations 20001 through 20175 for J-2s. J-3 production continued from C/N 2001, with a few given earlier unassigned J-3 C/Ns. J-3s assembled in Canada prefixed the C/N with the letter C, as C-1127 for CF-BIV (Fig. 3-4).

The nose and engine cowl of the J-3 were practically identical to those of the J-2. Gross weight of the J-3 Sport was 1000 pounds. Prices varied; in 1938 the cost was $1270, which dropped to $1249 and then $1098 in 1939. The all-time low J-3 price was $995 early in 1940.

Jack McNulty via John Underwood

3-4 A J-3 Sport assembled in Canada, identified by adding the letter C to the C/N, as C-1127. Note plain ailerons and large size of Canadian registration letters CF-BIV under the wing.

In a departure from its rule of different ATCs for different engines, the FAA allowed the installation of the new 40 Franklin 4AC-150 series 40 in the J-3 Sport, possibly because it was single-ignition and the J-3 Sport was already approved with single-ignition. The Franklin-powered J-3 on ATC A-660 became the J-3F-40 but the Continental version got no letter.

J-3C. When the twin-ignition Continental A-40-5 engine, which delivered 40 hp at 2575 rpm, was installed in the J-3, the plane became the J-3C, later J-3C-40, and received ATC A-691 on July 14, 1938. As more powerful Continentals became available, they were added to ATC A-691 even into postwar years as indicated below.

J-3C-40. Original powerplant for the J-3C was the dual-ignition A-40-5 engine (Fig. 3-5). Gross weight 1025 pounds. C/Ns started at 2325, with some skips to 2355, then all following were eligible.

3-5 A J-3C-40 C/N 2804, now with 40-hp Continental A-40-5 engine. This one has tail skid and short exhaust stacks. Note nonstandard black and cream color scheme even to using different color for the Cub logo on the tail, and the narrow skylight featured on all J-3 Cubs through 1941.

J-3C-50. The new Continental A-50 engine had a displacement of 171 cubic inches compared to 115 for the A-40, and delivered 50 hp at 1900 rpm. Exhaust stacks were on top of the cylinders (Figs. 3-6 and 3-7) and the additional 10 hp required an increase in the fuel capacity to 12 gallons. The single-ignition A-50-1 was not approved for the J-3C. The A-50 engine was fitted with air scoops over each pair of cylinders that were to become a distinctive J-3 feature. With this engine, the allowed gross weight was 1100 pounds. Initial price was $1499, soon lowered to $1368.

3-6 A J-3C-50 built under ATC-A691 with Frieze ailerons. Note top-side exhaust stacks on Continental A-50 engine and early J-3 Cub fuselage striping.

J-3C-65. Continental improved the A-50-4 and -5 engines to produce the A-65, which delivered 65 hp at 2350 rpm. The bore and stroke were the same as on the A-50, but the compression ratio was increased from 5.4:1 to 6.3:1. A-65s through -3 had the exhaust stacks on top of the cylinders as on the A-50, while later versions had them on the bottom (Fig. 3-8). Some A-65-8 engines retained the tapered crankshafts and removable metal hubs of the earlier models while others, designated A-65-8F, had flanged shafts.

Some post-WWII civil J-3C-65s converted from surplus navy NE-2s and army L-4Js used the Beech-Roby controllable propellers that were originally fitted to these models. Controllable-pitch propellers were desirable, especially on seaplanes, but were of little significance on airplanes under 125 hp. Maximum propeller efficiency for postwar J-3Cs was obtained from fixed-pitch metal propellers.

Gross weight for C/N 7842, 7845/7887 and 7912 and up was 1170 pounds. This could be increased to 1220 pounds provided the landing gear was reinforced. C/Ns prior to 7912 and not included above were allowed only 1100 pounds. Initial J-3C-65 price was $1598.

J-3C-75. In 1939 Continental increased the power of the A-65 to 75 hp at 2650 rpm and redesignated it the A-75. Existing A-65s could be converted and many were, but for Cubs, the power gained from this increased rpm was significantly offset by the decreased efficiency of the faster-turning propeller.

3-7 J-3C-50 Cub with top exhausts and separate right and left exhaust pipes, one with a carburetor heat muff and one with a cabin heat muff. Note nonstandard metal chock cord covers and bracket for wind-driven generator on landing gear.

Continental carried this practice even further, to the A-80, 80 hp at 2750 rpm, but this engine was not approved for J-3s on ATC A-691.

J-3C-85 and -90. These models were not official J-3 designations under ATC A-691. The installation of the Continental C-85, a 188 cubic-inch engine delivering 85 hp at 2575 rpm and the C-90, with 201 cubic inches delivering 90 hp at 2475 rpm, were approved for the J-3C on ATC A-691 when these engines became available after WWII.

3-8 A J-3C-65 with underside exhaust system. Right and left sides join inside cowling and discharge through single stack at bottom right. Note surrounding heat muff, cloth covers on shock absorbers, no brakes on wheels, and spring-leaf tailskid.

J-3F. Installation of the 150-cubic-inch Franklin 4AC-150, 50 hp at 2300 rpm, in the J-3 resulted in the designation J-3F. ATC A-692 was awarded July 14, 1938. The air scoops and exhaust stack arrangements were notably different than on the J-3C-50 and on, and provided the only external recognition point (Fig. 3-9).

Although the Franklin was a flat-four, air-cooled engine like the Continental, it was beam-mounted rather than radially-mounted, a detail not visible from outside the cowling.

The 50 hp of the Franklin 4AC-150 Series 50 was reflected in the airplane designation J-3F-50.

The same C/Ns listed for the J-3C-40 were eligible for the J-3F-50, which also started with 12 gallon fuel capacity. Gross weight was 1100 pounds and initial cost as $1548.

J-3F-60. By turning the Franklin 4AC-150 at 2400 rpm it became the Series 60. Gross weight was the same as for the J-3F-50. Actual cost is not avail-

3-9 A J-3F-50 with top-side exhausts on Franklin engine with air scoop for heat muff around left-side exhaust of two separate systems.

able. Recognition features of the J-3F-50 and -60 were the shape of the cylinder rocker box covers, generally triangular in shape, and topside exhaust stacks (Fig. 3-10).

J-3F-65. Installation of the 65-hp Franklin 4AC-176B-2 engine resulted in the J-3F-65, the most common F-model. This larger-displacement engine had bottom exhaust stacks and square rocker boxes (Fig. 3-11) that were virtually indistinguishable from those of the A-65. Gross weight was initially the same 1100 pounds as the J-3F-50 and -60, but could be increased to 1170 pounds when the wing struts and attachment fittings were strengthened.

J-3P-50. The J-3P, with the 50-hp Lenape "Papoose" radial engine, was the least-produced version of the J-3 Cub, with approximately 30 built (Fig. 3-12). Like the Szekely, the name of the Lenape engine has long been mispronounced. It is Lah-na-pay, not Le-nape or Le-nap. The letter L would have been logical to identify a Lenape engine in a Cub but L was already committed to Lycoming, so Piper picked P-for-Papoose as the identifying letter.

Although new in name, the engine itself was not. In 1938 Lenape Aircraft & Motors Inc., of Matawan, New Jersey, acquired the assets of the Aeroma-

3-10 Closeup of Franklin 4AC-150 Series 50 engine in J-3F-50 with top-side exhaust. Note triangular shape of rocker box covers on 50 and 60 series engines and air scoops inboard of the exhausts.

rine Plane and Motor Corporation of Keyport, New Jersey, whose AR-3 three-cylinder radial had been used in the Taylor F-2 in 1935. The AR-3 was put back in production by Lenape. The first few were sold as AR-3s, but the designation was soon changed to LM-3.

The AR-3/LM-3 was not notably successful. One of its drawbacks was rough running, sometimes shaking the airplane so much that the pilot could not read the instruments. Power was 50 hp at 2200 rpm. The J-3P received ATC A-695 on August 23, 1938. Fuel capacity was 12 gallons, gross weight was 1100 pounds, and the price was $1495.

The J-3P was nearly the last American lightplane to be certificated with a radial engine under 125 hp. The development of small flat (or opposed) engines was so rapid and successful in the late 1930s that they drove the rough-running small radials from the market. Some existing designs like the Monocoupe and the Bellanca Cruisaire that had been using 5-cylinder radials converted to flat engines.

The only notable performance by a J-3P was a 63-hour non-stop flight from Newark, New Jersey to Miami, Florida, and return. Refueling en-route was accomplished by picking up cans of gas from cars speeding down airport runways. The 2339-mile flight was made in May 1938, long before the L-3P was certificated, by C/N 2080, NX20280. This was the first L-3P and was

3-11 Closeup of J-3F-65 shows underside exhaust and square rocker box covers of Franklin 4AC-176B-2 engine. Right and left-side exhaust systems join behind engine and exit through a single stack as on the J-3C-65.

used by Lenape as a test vehicle. The out-and-back distance probably still stands as a record for a Cub.

J-3L. Lycoming entered the small-engine field and was soon a major producer along with Continental and Franklin. Piper naturally offered this engine for the J-3 as the J-3L. The beam-mounted Lycoming O-145 had 145 cubic inch displacement. Power started at 50 hp and advanced to 80, but not all versions were certificated in J-3Ls.

At first, the designation was plain J-3L, but engines of different power were soon reflected by suffix letters to the airplane designation. A recognition point for all J-3Ls was a triangular indentation in the cowling behind the engine similar to that on J-2s and J-3s with Continental A-40 engines (Fig. 3-13).

J-3L-50. The J-3L-50, with a single-ignition Lycoming O-145-A1 delivering 50 hp at 2300 rpm, received ATC A-698 on September 17, 1938. Gross weight was 1100 pounds and fuel capacity was 12 gallons. The first J-3L-50 was C/N 2490, NC21678, and price ranged from $1298 to $1499.

3-12 Rarest of the J-3 Cubs was the J-3P with Lenape Papoose radial engine. This one has a nonstandard color scheme and fuselage stripe.

3-13 J-3L-65 shows the triangular indentation in the cowling behind the Lycoming O-145 engine that was a feature of all J-3Ls. This view shows the three-piece windshield and center-section detail of the 1937–1942 J-3 Cubs.

J-3L-55. An alternate engine was the dual-ignition Lycoming O-145-A2 that delivered 55 hp at 2300 rpm. The O-145-A3 had the same power but was 15 pounds heavier because of accessories.

J-3L-65. The improved O-145-B1 delivered 65 hp at 2550 rpm and became, along with the O-145-B3, the most widely used O-145 in the J-3L. The J-3L-65 was easily distinguished from the -50 and -55 models by the external exhaust stacks entering the nose behind the engine as on the J-3C-65 (Fig. 3-14). Price of the J-3L-65 was $1598.

J-3X. One J-3C-65, C/N 9110, NX42111, was fitted with an experimental cantilever wing in November 1944, and was redesignated J-3X.

E.M. Sommerich

3-14 The right and left side exhausts of the J-3L-65 joined behind the engine to form a single stack as on the J-3C-65 and the J-3F-65, but the triangular cowling indentation was retained.

4

Other Cub models
1938–1942

With the J-3 well established as its main product line, Piper expanded its market by developing several new models. Some of these aircraft became significant production models while others were one-only prototypes.

The J-4 Cub Coupe series

Late in 1937 Hanford Eckman, Piper's plant manager, suggested upgrading the basic Cub for the private owner, rather than the trainer market. Piper was reluctant to approve this concept but finally consented with the admonition that it be more comfortable than the J-3.

Work got underway on a side-by-side two seater that was promptly and logically named the "Cub Coupe" because of the seating arrangement. The wings were identical to the J-3 except for adaptation to the revised fuselage structure. The wider landing gear now used spring shock absorbers instead of rubber cord. Fuel was carried in a 16-gallon nose tank as on the J-3. Besides the fatter fuselage, the contour of the rudder also was changed by rounding out the trailing edge. Entry was by means of a forward-hinged door on the right side of the fuselage.

The engine chosen for the prototpye was an odd choice, the unproven but promising Skymotor. This was an inverted four-cylinder, in-line air-cooled design (Fig. 4-1). Production Cub Coupes all used the well-established flat-four engines. Skymotors was a new company formed in Milwaukee, Wisconsin, in 1938. Its first engines were built by the Milwaukee Parts Company,

4-1 The first J-4 Cub Coupe was flown briefly with the experimental inverted four-cylinder in-line Skymotor engine. This is a later J-4A C/N 4-757, with experimental license used to continue testing of the Skymotor after the prototype was fitted with the Continental A-50. Note the name "Skymotor 60" on the nose.

builders of the famous Tank engine of a decade before, an air-cooled conversion of the Curtiss OX-5. On the original Type Certificate for the Skymotor, issued in 1938, the engine was erroneously identified as a Tank. This error was corrected on a revised 1939 Certificate, but the word Tank had already gotten into Piper paperwork and still misleads historians.

In spite of all its changes, plus having been developed by a new designer, the Cub Coupe did not get a new letter model number. It retained the J, now accepted as meaning Jamouneau, with one digit added to become J-4. However, an entirely new C/N series was adopted, starting with 4-400.

J-4C(1). Certification of the production Cub Coupe was obtained under ATC A-703 on October 26, 1938, using a 50-hp Continental A-50-1 engine (Fig. 4-2). Single-ignition engines were still legal when the J-4 appeared. For $52 additional, the buyer could have dual ignition. After August 1, 1941, single-ignition engines became illegal for all U.S. commercial airplanes that had not been certificated with single-ignition engines before that date. Eligible serial numbers were 4-400 and up, which would indicate that the Skymotor engine of the prototype, C/N 4-400, had been replaced with an A-50.

4-2 Initial production model of the Cub Coupe was designated J-4C for its Continental engine, but the letter was soon dropped. This one had a minor accident; note broken propeller and windshield.

At first, the designation was J-4C to reflect the Continental engine, as was done with the J-3, but a change to the 65-hp Continental A-65 resulted in a designation change to J-4A, so the A-50 version became plain J-4. Basic price was $1995.

J-4A. Added to ATC A-703 on July 25, 1939, the more powerful 65-hp J-4A was simply a refined J-4 with such added features as cabin furnishings and an optional 9-gallon auxiliary fuel tank in the left wing. A second door in the left side of the cabin was offered as an option. Electrical systems for instrument flying lights, even landing lights, could be installed. Power came from a wind-driven generator installed under the belly.

Eligible C/Ns were 4-400 and up, meaning that earlier Coupes with A-50 engines could be converted to J-4As on the same ATC. The first J-4A built was C/N 4-490, NC22824, and added to ATC A-703 on March 4, 1939.

The J-4As using the new Continental A-65-1 and -3 engines with overhead exhaust systems had open cowlings with air scoops as on equivalent J-3Cs (Fig. 4-3). Some J-4As with A-65-8 engines having underside exhausts also had open cowlings, but the new exhaust arrangement allowed some to be delivered with closed cowlings in a move to match equivalent models by Aeronca and Taylorcraft.

4-3 Cub Coupe J-5A with early top-exhaust Continental A-65 engine. Note different three-piece windshield pattern than on J-3, and large size of Canadian registration letters required until well after WWII.

In using the J-5A designation, the Cub Coupe broke with the J-3 tradition of using the letter following the number to identify the engine. The letters may have been intended to indicate sequence of development but didn't hold to it exactly in the case of the J-4 series.

J-4B. Essentially a J-4A but with a 60-hp Franklin 4AC-171 engine (Fig. 4-4). ATC A-708 was awarded March 16, 1939 for C/Ns 4-400 and up, meaning that early Model 4 airframes could be re-engined with Franklins and licensed under ATC A-708 instead of A-703. The first J-4B built was C/N 4-481, NX21696, rolled out on February 13, 1939. Basic price was $1848. Open and closed cowlings were available.

J-4C(2). Because it had been used on the early Coupes with A-50 engines, the J-4C designation was not used later to indicate sequential development.

J-4D. This designation was not used for a production model, but is believed to apply to C/N 4-408, NK22781, tested with a 50-hp Lenape "Papoose" radial engine early in 1939.

J-4E. The J-4E, licensed under ATC-740 on April 28, 1941, was the J-4A airframe with a 75-hp Continental A-75-9 engine (Fig. 4-5). This delivered 75 hp at 2600 rpm. The A-75 was simply the A-65 fitted with higher compression, revised carburetor jets, and turning a smaller propeller faster to get the extra 10 hp. However, decreased efficiency of the faster propeller offset some of the increase. Original engine cowlings were open, but closed cowlings were an available option. Eligible C/Ns were 4-1378, 4-1385, and up. Initial price was $2395, raised to $2575 in July 1941. The last Cub Coupe built was a J-4E, delivered December 11, 1941.

4-4 Different exhaust stack arrangement of Franklin 60 engine allowed the J-4B Cub Coupe to be fitted with a closed cowling, the first used on a production Piper airplane.

4-5 J-4E Cub Coupe had a Continental A-75 engine under a closed cowl similar to that of the J-4B and the subsequent J-4F with the 65-hp Lycoming O-145.

J-4F. The highest designated Cub Coupe model was the J-4F. Again, this was like the J-4A but with the 65-hp Lycoming O-145-B1 or B3 engine (Fig. 4-6). The J-4F received ATC A-721 on March 22, 1940. Eligible C/Ns were 4-828 and up. Initial price was $1910, soon raised to $1948.

J-4RX. One J-4E was fitted with the experimental Rose Slotted Wing. It was given a new C/N, RX-2, and registration NX22941.

4-6 Cub Coupe J-4F Lycoming engine was outwardly similar to other Coupes with closed cowlings. This one has been fitted with a ground-adjustable Friedman-Burnham propeller.

The J-5 Cub Cruiser series

To increase the earning power of the Cub for commercial operators and provide an extra seat for private owners, Piper introduced the three-seat J-5 Cub Cruiser in December 1939. Two passengers sat side-by-side on a single board seat behind the pilot, who sat alone. Dual controls could be fitted for two-seat training. Since the pilot was moved forward slightly, the traditional Cub nose fuel tank was replaced by an 18-gallon tank in the right wing with a 1-gallon header tank in the nose. An auxiliary 9-gallon tank was optional for the left wing.

Entry to front and rear seats was through a large hinge-forward door on the right side. The rudder had the rounded shape of the J-4, but the landing gear reverted to the J-3 type with external shock absorbers. The wing was the same as the J-3 and J-4 except for minor changes for fuselage attachment and accommodation of fuel tanks. Suffix letter designations were sequential except for some modified as prototypes for the military L-14. Production of the J-5 Cruiser continued into 1942. A total of 1507 were built.

J-5. Only two Cub Cruisers carried the plain J-5 designation: the prototypes that started a new C/N series at 5-1 and 5-2, NX24573 and NX26071. These were used to obtain certification for the production model, which was awarded ATC A-725 on April 13, 1940.

J-5A. First production model of the J-5, used the 75 hp Continental A-75-8 engines and open cowling (Fig. 4-7). Eligible C/Ns 5-2 and up. From C/N 5-784 and up, the fuel capacity was increased to 25 gallons by adding a 7-gallon header tank. Initial price was $1798, raised to $1833 in July 1940, and to $1995 in April 1941.

4-7 Three-seat J-5A Cub Cruiser was essentially a J-3 with a widened fuselage. Standard color was International Orange with black trim. Note wide hinge-forward passenger door.

J-5A-80. Installation of an 80 hp Continental A-80 engine, 80 hp at 2700 rpm was approved for ATC A-725 on July 31, 1942, but was not a production installation.

J-5A-85. Although not used on prewar Cubs, the Continental C-85-12, a 188 cubic inch engine delivering its 85 hp at a much more efficient propeller speed of 2575 rpm, was added to the J-5A on ATC A-725, but was not a production installation.

J-5A-90. The later Continental C-90-8F, 90 hp at 2475 rpm, was also approved for the J-5A and J-5B airplanes on ATC A-725.

J-5B. The J-5B marked a switch in FAA certification policy. A different engine, the geared Lycoming GO-145-62 75 hp at 3200 rpm, was added to ATC A-725 for a Cub Cruiser variant designated J-5B (Fig. 4-8). The test J-5B was C/N 5-106, NC28071, rolled out June 15, 1940, with a 65-hp Lycoming O-145-B engine. The first production J-5B was C/N 5-617, NC35273. Initial price was $2150.

4-8 J-5B Cub Cruiser used the 75-hp geared Lycoming GO-145C-2 engine. Note greater distance from cylinders to propeller because of gearbox on front of engine.

J-5C. Early in 1942 Piper brought out an improved Cub Cruiser, the J-5C, powered with a 100-hp Lycoming O-235 engine under a closed cowling and with an improved landing gear having internal shock absorbers (Fig. 4-9). One J-5C, C/N 1835, was licensed after WWII on Memo Approval 2-563, but this was soon added to ATC A-725. Initial fuel capacity was 20 gallons, 18 in a right wing tank and 2 in a nose header tank. An 18-gallon left wing tank was optional.

Published figures differ as to the number of J-3Cs built, but the accepted figure is 35. Eligible C/Ns were 5-1309, NX41333, and 5-1388 and up. In spite of all the J-5Cs having been built early in 1942, that model was not added to ATC A-725 until December 21, 1942. With the U.S. now in WWII and light civil aircraft production curtailed, it is a puzzle as to what market absorbed the J-5C production.

J-5CA. One J-5C, C/N 5-1386, NX41551, was modified as a civil prototype of the U.S. Navy HE-1/AE-1 ambulance plane. See page 56.

J-5CO. One J-5C, C/N 5-1387, NX41552, was modified as a civil prototype of the U.S. Army L-14. See page 52.

Piper via Clyde R. Smith, Sr.

4-9 The J-5C Cruiser of 1942 had a 100-hp Lycoming O-235C engine under a closed cowl and the landing gear shock absorbers moved inside the fuselage as on the J-4 Coupe.

Nonproduction Cub models—1939–1942

Piper developed some new designs that were considered for production and should not be considered as pure experimentals like the J-4RX. These are described below.

Model P-1 Cub Clipper. In 1939 Ray Applegate, a designer-builder, trucked a home-built amphibian to Lock Haven and interested Piper in producing it. It had some good features, such as an all-metal hull, but Piper engineers saw much room for improvement. A set of J-3 wings was fitted, along with a 60-hp Lenape Papoose radial engine (Fig. 4-10) replacing the original Essex automobile engine. Applegate's original amphibian was already registered as NX17866, C/N 1. Piper tested NX17866, replaced the Lenape engine with a 75-hp Continental and then a 90-hp Franklin 4AC-190-E2 and made modifications to the hull and wing bracing (Fig. 4-11). Piper then built a second prototype, Piper C/N P-1, NX27960, with a 130-hp Franklin 4AC-238 engine (Fig. 4-12).

The amphibian was briefly publicized as the "Cub Clipper," but was not put into production.

Model P-2. In 1941 Piper looked toward improved Cub variants for the private-owner market. Also, the company decided that the J-designation should end with the J-5 that was then in production.

4-10 The Applegate-Piper "Cub Clipper" as originally flown with 60-hp Lenape Papoose engine. Note strut arrangement for rubber wing floats and that landing gear rotates aft for retraction.

4-11 Second Cub Clipper prototype with Continental A-75 engine, J-3 Cub wing, and revised hull. Landing gear is now ahead of the wing struts and retracts forward.

Richard E. Smith

4-12 Second Cub Clipper prototype with Franklin engine shows the unique gulling of the rear portion of the wing root and the rear-view windows for the pilot's cabin.

The next Cub variant was designated P-2, P-for-Piper (Fig. 4-13). It was a shortened J-3 Cub with tandem seating but with a forward-opening door on the right side as on the J-4 Cub Coupe. The vertical tail had greatly enlarged fin area, less rudder balance area, and a curved rudder trailing edge as on the J-4 and J-5. The enclosed engine was originally a 60-hp Franklin 4AC-171, but was soon replaced by 75-hp Continental A-75-8.

The one-only P-2 NX33281, C/N O built in 1941, was never certificated. It flew on an experimental license in the National Air Shows Organization in the late 1940s.

Model P-4. This was a 4-seat development of the P-2, NX30300, C/N 1. It was powered by a 120-hp Lycoming O-290 engine. The P-4 was never certificated, but some of its details were combined with the J-5C Cub Cruiser airframe to produce the HE-1 navy ambulance plane of 1942–43.

4-13 The one-only Piper P-2 was essentially a cleaned-up J-3 Cub with some J-4 Cub Coupe details like closed engine cowling and a hinge-forward door, seen here when used for air show work in 1949.

5

The Cub
goes to war

While Piper J-3C Cubs under the U.S. Army designation of L-4 saw extensive action in WWII and into the Korean War, their entry into military service was not easy. They got in virtually by the back door, with a major shove by John E.P. Morgan, a Piper board member and friend of high government officials.

In May 1940, W.T. Piper attended a meeting of all U.S. airplane manufacturers called in Washington, D.C. This was to bring the industry up to date on President Franklin Roosevelt's call for production of 50,000 airplanes a year. The lightplane manufacturers asked if there would be a place in the program for lightplanes. They were told that there would not, at least as far as the U.S. Army Air Corps was concerned.

Some entirely unofficial activity followed. In 1941 when the army held maneuvers, it asked the air corps (by now renamed U.S. Army Air Forces, or USAAF) for some observation planes, but the USAAF could not spare any. Recalling entirely unofficial demonstrations of lightplane capability at various army bases in 1940, Assistant Secretary of War Robert A. Lovett wrote to Morgan, who was then representing Aeronca and Taylorcraft as well as Piper in his campaign to sell military lightplanes, suggesting the use of lightplanes in the maneuvers. The manufacturers readily agreed. In the absence of any contract, Piper provided eight radio-equipped J-3C-65 Cubs while Aeronca and Taylorcraft provided two 65-hp tandem-seat models each.

After brief demonstrations of the J-3s capabilities at Ft. Riley, Kansas, on June 12–14, the loaned lightplanes joined full-scale army maneuvers at Manchester, Tennessee, on June 18. This first operation was not successful, but did impress the field commanders with the utility of the lightplane. Its slow speed enabled it to fly low and slow for a look at what was hidden under the trees, something that the bigger O-types could not do. It could also land on roads and in small clearings to deliver personnel and to act as an aerial dispatch motorcycle (Fig. 5-1).

5-1 One of the civil J-3C-65s that Piper pilots flew in various 1941 U.S. Army maneuvers being refueled at a country store's gas pumps. Note the cavalry in the background, the "War Games" cross on the fuselage, and the "Grasshopper" insignia originated by Piper people.

This activity earned the little airplane the nickname "Grasshopper," which originated in a casual remark by Cavalry Major General Innis P. Swift to Piper pilot Henry S. Wann. On July 15, 1942, Wann was directed to fly a message from Biggs Field, Ft. Bliss, Texas, to Gen. Swift at his field headquarters. After observing Wann's rough landing in an unimproved field, the general told Wann: "You looked like a damn grasshopper when you landed that thing out there in those boondocks and bounced around."

Later, after Wann had flown back to Biggs Field, Gen. Swift wanted him and his airplane again. He sent a message to Biggs: "Send Grasshopper." This first actual use of the name baffled personnel at Biggs until Wann explained it to them.

Someone in the Piper group quickly dreamed up a grasshopper insignia and painted it on the sides of the civil-marked Cubs. Piper picked up further on the idea and had enameled grasshopper lapel pins made and distributed.

Army personnel not connected with the operation of the planes were at a loss as to how to process their maintenance and the feeding and housing of their crews. During another maneuver at Fort Bliss, the lightplanes were on loan again. General Arnold of the USAAF signed an order for assignment of the planes and their crews to the 2nd Cavalry, but the army general commanding did not fully comply. After having to stay at a hotel in town at their own expense, the pilots were understandably unhappy. Morgan telephoned his friend Lovett. Lovett then called the cavalry general, and the lightplane crews immediately got quarters and messing on post.

In the meantime, the lightplanes did a fantastic job and as many influential officers as possible were given rides. One Lt. Col. Dwight D. Eisenhower, a pilot himself, liked the Cub so well that he would borrow one for a little off-duty recreational flying.

The army wanted the lightplanes for still more maneuvers but the manufacturers were getting tired of supplying free airplanes and paying for their crews and maintenance with no prospect of sales to the military. With no channel for the army ground forces to buy airplanes on their own, Morgan suggested that the army rent the planes. After some head-scratching, the idea was approved. Finally, late in 1941, the USAAF was persuaded to procure four each service test airplanes from Taylorcraft (YO-57), Aeronca (YO-58), and Piper (YO-59). The letter Y identified service test status. The lightplanes were now officially "in" (Fig. 5-2).

Subsequent production, after a 1942 designation change from O-for-Observation to L-for-Liaison, favored Piper. Some 5673 O-59/L-4s were built by Piper compared to 1941 O-57/L-2s by Taylorcraft and 1039 O-58/L-3s by Aeronca. The navy followed the army lead and ordered Cubs as described under U.S. Navy Cubs.

Of the three light L-types, only Piper's L-4 series was sent overseas during the war. These Pipers served in all theatres in a great variety of roles and ingenious new ways were found in which to launch and retrieve them when no proper fields existed. Initial coloring was the standard army olive drab on top and sides with gray undersides, but by 1944 the late models were being delivered in all-silver finish. Some L-4s used in the Korean War readopted camouflage and were painted olive drab all over.

After the war, surplus L-4s could be licensed as civil airplanes under the prewar ATC for the J-3C Cub. Many owners modified their L-4s back to J-3 standard, but some retained the rear windows after modifying the rear seat.

5-2 The first Piper YO-59s were delivered to the army in time to participate in some of the 1941 war games. This one is 42-461, delivered September 17, 1941, and photographed at Hawkins Field, Jackson, Mississippi, on September 17.

U.S. Army Cub procurement—1941–1945

All Cub production for the army was at Lock Haven. The only differences from the civil model were reversion to wooden wing spars plus furnishing and equipment changes specified by the customer. Army serial numbers will be found in Appendix II.

YO-59. Because the YO-59s ordered were stock models, delivery was almost immediate, with the first on September 17, 1941, and YO-59s participated in the late 1941 war games. Communication equipment was one battery-powered commercial RCA AVT 2300-6200KC radio transmitter and one RCA AVR-20A receiver. The civil Continental A-65 engine was given the army designation of O-170-3, the O identifying an opposed type, the 170 the displacement to the nearest five cubic inches, and the -3 the second army version of the A-65. (Army engines had odd-dash numbers; navy engines had even dash numbers.)

Unit cost was $2230. In most of its airplane procurements, the army bought only the airframe from the manufacturer and provided him with the engine, instruments, and military equipment as government-furnished equipment, or GFE. In the case of the early grasshoppers, the army bought the complete package from the manufacturer, including commercial radio, and added very little on its own.

The Y-for-service test designation was soon dropped and the planes became plain O-59 before being re-designated L-4 early in 1942.

After official names were given to U.S. military airplanes in October 1941, the O-59 shared the name "Grasshopper" with the O-57 and the O-58. Later, under its L-4 designation, the O-59 Cub earned its own nickname—"Maytag Messerschmitt."

O-59. The performance of the four YO-59s resulted in an order for 140 production O-59s (Fig. 5-3), with first delivery on November 28, 1941.

These O-59s were more completely equipped as military airplanes, with built-in 6-volt electrical systems and a reel for the long trailing wire antenna of the commercial radios. The antenna was pulled to its extended position by a rubber drogue through a fairlead on top of the rudder. Unit cost complete of an O-59 was $2230.

5-3 The production O-59s were stock Model J-3C-65 Cubs with added military radio equipment. This is 42-7815 photographed while under test at Wright Field. Drag cone at top of rudder pulls low-frequency radio antenna to full length behind the plane.

O-59A. A total of 948 improved O-59As were ordered. The major change was to revise the rear cabin to allow the observer to turn his seat to face backward and to improve his visibility by adding a large transparent area to the fuselage immediately behind the wing (Fig. 5-4). This change was requested by the army and was also accomplished on the Taylorcraft O-57A-L-2A and the Aeronca O-58A/L-3A. Piper worked out its modification on a civil J-3, NX41555, C/N 8175. Powerplant and radio were as on the O-59/L-4.

Deliveries began on February 16, 1942. The unit cost complete of $2154 reflected the price reduction resulting from the larger production order. The designation was changed to L-4A after 649 O-59As had been delivered.

5-4 First notable change to the J-3C Cub for military use was the added glasswork behind the rear cockpit of the O-59A, soon redesignated L-4A. This one, photographed in England,later has radio with a fixed antenna extending to the top of the vertical fin.

L-4B. Still with O-170-3 engines, 980 duplicates of the O-59A/L-4A were ordered for the field artillery, with deliveries beginning on July 20, 1942 (Fig. 5-5). The higher series letter resulted from minor airframe improvements. A carburetor air filter was fitted into the bottom of the cowling nose bowl after delivery (Fig. 5-6). Also, the factory did not install the radio and other military equipment and there was no electrical system. Unit cost of the L-4B, including engine and other equipment supplied by Piper, was $2163. Added GFE brought the total to $2421.

L-4C through L-4G. These were existing civil J-3, J-4, and J-5 Cubs purchased from private owners in 1942. See Drafted Cubs, page 59.

L-4H. Improved versions of the L-4B were the 1801 L-4Hs, still with O-170-3 engines and no electrical system. Improvements included a revised hydraulic brake system, military instruments, and a gross weight increase to 1220 pounds. The L-4H could be distinguished from the L-4B externally by a new one-piece windshield instead of the original three-piece unit (Fig. 5-7). Deliveries began on June 30, 1943, and some 1301 L-4Hs were shipped to the European and African theatres from 1943 into 1945. Unit prices rose only slightly for the first 1301, to a total of $2461. The final 500 were listed at $2654.

L-4I. The army/air force does not use I as a series letter.

L-4J. The final production L-4s were the 1680 L-4Js, with deliveries beginning October 25, 1944. These were outwardly identical to the L-4Hs but

5-5 This early L-4B is an oddity in that it was delivered in over-all silver finish while later models were delivered in camouflage into 1944. Number 49 has not yet been fitted with a carburetor air filter.

5-6 An L-4B after being fitted with a carburetor air filter that projects well ahead of the cowling. Note retention of the prewar three-piece J-3 Cub windshield.

5-7 The first Piper L-4H, 43-29247, was also the first L-4 to be delivered with the revised U.S. star insignia incorporating white rectangles and a red border. The red was changed to blue in September 1942.

were to have controllable-pitch Beech-Roby propellers. These were controllable through a torque rod operated by a hand crank on the left cabin wall just above the fuel shut-off. The propeller had a pitch adjustment range of six degrees from HIGH RPM to LOW RPM through 7½ turns of the crank.

Apparently the controllable propellers were not very successful, for Army Technical Order 01-140DC-1, covering the L-4 series, states that only some L-4Js were so equipped. All of the available L-4J photos show only wooden fixed-pitch propellers.

The first 800 L-4Js had the same unit costs as the last L-4Hs; the final 880 cost $2701. At war's end, the last 270 L-4Js on order were cancelled. A total of 794 L-4Js were shipped to Europe and Africa in 1944 and 1945.

L-4K. No L-4s were built under this designation, but 15 mixed L-4As, Bs, and Hs were redesignated as such in the late 1940s, and some served in the Korean War.

TL-4. Some L-4s were equipped specifically for glider towing under the unofficial designation of TL-4 (T-for-Tug). Ordinarily, the T-prefix identified an airplane of a different category modified for use as a trainer.

YL-14. The military Cub that was ordered into production as the L-14 in 1945 evolved from two civil prototypes. To meet an army requirement for an L-plane with higher performance than the L-4, Piper converted a J-5C, C/N 5-1387, NX41552, under the designation J-5CO (O-for-Observation). Major changes were to cut the aft fuselage superstructure near the wing down to the upper longerons to provide a more extensive glass area than on the L-4. Originally, the landing gear was as on the J-5C, but to absorb the impact of hard landings, a long-stroke landing gear with shock struts attached to the upper longeron was adopted (Fig. 5-8). The engine was still the 100-hp Lycoming O-235.

Piper via Richard E. Smith

5-8 Piper modified J-5C NX41552, C/N 5-1387, to a prototype of a larger and more powerful liaision plane for the Army, the L-14. The company-owned airplane was designated J-5CO and featured a modified rear fuselage. This photo was taken before the addition of wing flaps and slots and long-stroke landing gear.

At first, the wing was standard Cub, but was soon modified, first to have trailing-edge flaps, a first for Piper, then full-span slots built into the leading edge. The elevators were balanced, another first for Piper. No army orders resulted from this.

In 1945, a second prototype was converted from J-5C C/N 5-1387, NX33529, under the Piper designation of L-4X (Fig. 5-9). In anticipation of a following military series, the C/N was changed to 5-3001. Major changes were a 125-hp Lycoming O-290-A engine and a higher rear turtledeck with revised glasswork. Wing slots and flaps were retained, but the inner three feet of the slots were later removed.

The army, now seriously interested, ordered 850 production L-14s with 130-hp military Lycoming O-240-3 engines. Five of these were to be service test YL-14 models. The two prototypes were modified to production standard and delivered in May 1945 as the first two YL-14s. Oddly, they and the

5-9 Second prototype for the L-14 was another J-5C, this one designated L-4X and given a new serial number. Compare rear fuselage and glasswork with J-5CO model.

following three YL-14s delivered in June, all carried civil registrations and had no military markings. The glasswork of the YL-14 (Fig. 5-10) was like that of the J-5CO, but the structure was hinged and could be raised to admit a stretcher case as on the navy HE-1/AE-1 variant of the J-5C (see page 40).

The end of the war in August 1945, ended the army's interest in the L-14. Nine then on the production line were completed as civil airplanes, the L-14 having already received ATC A-760 on July 31, 1945.

TG-8. The oddest modification of a Cub for the military was the TG-8 Training Glider. Because the army was dissatisfied with the high-performance civil sailplane designs used in its initial glider training program of 1941–1942, the Taylorcraft people came up with a unique quick solution.

They took a stock Taylorcraft tandem similar to the L-2, removed the engine section at the firewall and added a new bolt-on nose that housed an additional person and a set of controls. In the absence of a propeller, a much shorter landing gear could be used. The only aerodynamic change was to add glider-type spoilers to the upper wing surface to allow steep landing approaches without excessive speed.

Aeronca and Piper followed the Taylorcraft lead, and each received an army order for three prototypes—Aeronca TG-5, Taylorcraft TG-6, and Piper TG-8 (Fig. 5-11). These were followed by a contract to each firm for 250 production models. For these, Piper established a new C/N series, G-1 through G-253.

Piper via Roger Peperell

5-10 The first production article of five YL-14s delivered to the U.S. Army. This has more glasswork than the J-5CO prototype, plus fairings on the long shock absorber struts.

Piper via Clyde Smith, Sr.

5-11 The Piper TG-8 glider for the army was a J-3C airframe with a new nose structure bolted onto the original motor mount fittings and equipped with a third set of flight controls. Note shortened landing gear and hinge-up canopy for the front cockpit.

After the war the soaring movement snapped up all of the sailplane-type training gliders that had been made since 1943, but had no use for the lower-performance three-seaters. Although Piper had obtained Glider Type Certificate GTC-10 for the TG-8 on August 19, 1942, there was no civil demand for it. That was not the end of them, however. All three designs could be modified easily back to standard-category light airplanes with normal noses and landing gear. One requirement of the re-conversion was to deactivate the wing spoilers.

U.S. Navy Cubs—1942–1945

The navy followed the army lead in buying J-3C Cubs, but designated them as primary trainers. Later, the navy had Piper develop a specialized aerial ambulance version of the J-5C Cub Cruiser.

NE-1. The 230 NE-1s (N for Trainer, E for Piper in navy designations) were given a single block of navy serial numbers but were not built under a normal navy contract. Instead, the navy simply took over Piper's on-hand stock of J-3C-65s and those on the production line. The engines were given the army designation of O-170-3. Deliveries were in "Cub yellow" which was also the standard color for navy primary trainers ("Yellow Perils") at the time. The final 40 NE-1s broke the steady sequence of J-3 C/Ns. They carried C/Ns 8277-1 through 8277-40 located between C/Ns 8276 and 8278.

Some of the navy planes even retained the civil Cub logo on the tail (Fig. 5-12). A few used as utility planes attached to operational squadrons in U.S. coastal zones in 1942 were camouflaged and upgraded to have electrical systems, night lights, and radios.

NE-2. Only 10 of 20 NE-2s ordered were delivered. These were L-4Js transferred from the army, and had controllable-pitch propellers (Fig. 5-13). As transfers from the army, the NE-2s had army olive drab and gray coloring and the engine was the army O-170-3. Some NE-2s were operated on floats.

HE-1/AE-1. The navy ordered 100 variants of the J-5C Cub Cruiser as HE-1 ambulance planes (H-for-Hospital). Like the J-5C, the HE-1 could carry three, but when equipped as an ambulance, it carried only the pilot and one stretcher patient. To accommodate the patient, the full length of the turtledeck aft of the wing hinged upward to allow the stretcher to be put into the cabin from behind (Fig. 5-14). The navy version of the civil Lycoming O-235-B engine was O-235-2.

Early HE-1 deliveries were painted over-all Cub yellow, the prevailing standard for navy ambulance planes, but the final ones were all silver.

In 1943, the designation was changed from HE-1 to AE-1 (A-for-Ambulance) since H was to be used for the new helicopters (Fig. 5-15). After the

5-12 U.S. Navy NE-1 trainers were stock J-3C Cubs taken over from civil production, even to the Cub logo. This one was photographed early in 1943, just as the star insignia was being added to the fuselages of uncamouflaged airplanes and the upper right and lower left wing stars were being removed.

5-13 This navy NE-2, 29669, is one of 10 L-4Js acquired from the U.S. Army and retains army coloring and the controllable-pitch propellers that were to have been standard equipment on L-4Js.

war, surplus AE-1s could be licensed as civil airplanes under the prewar ATC for the Piper J-5 Cub Cruiser series.

XLNP-1. The navy ordered three TG-8 gliders as XLNP-1, the LN standing for training glider and the P for Piper instead of the E used for the NEs and HEs. Only the three were procured. Instead, the navy bought nine experimental equivalents and 25 production articles from Taylorcraft as XLNT-1 and LNT-1.

Piper

5-14 Piper easily converted the J-5C Cub Coupe model into the HE-1 ambulance plane for the U.S. Navy. The external hinge allows the rear turtledeck to hinge upward to allow the insertion of a stretcher patient.

William T. Larkins

5-15 When the navy adopted the type letter H to identify helicopters in 1942, the H-for-Hospital designation of the HE-1 was changed to AE-1, A-for-Ambulance.

Drafted Cubs—1945

It is well known that the U.S. Army drafted many transport planes from the airlines and from the manufacturers right off the factory floors. However, it also drafted (actually purchased at current market prices) many smaller types for communications and utility use.

The government acquired some 118 Cubs of various models this way. Lightplanes had flight characteristics more like the cargo gliders that would go into combat, so the army used most of its drafted Cubs for pre-glider flight training under the L-for-Liaison designation because of their similarity to the existing L-types. Student pilots learned the basics of flying in the Cubs, then moved on to gliders to master their particular characteristics. Some Cub models were evaluated in the C-for-Cargo (transport) category, but were re-designated as various L-4s.

Unfortunately for historians, none of these underwent the normal military evaluation as new models; they were simply acquired to put to work. Official photographs were not taken and wartime restrictions prevented the interested photo collectors who saw them from taking pictures even though no military security was involved.

These military designations and the number taken from the civilian fleet are as follows:

L-4C. Ten J-3L-65.

L-4D. Five J-3F-65.

L-4E. Sixteen J-4E Cub Coupes.

L-4F. Forty-five J-5A, plus one UC-83 redesignated.

L-4G. Forty-one J-5B.

UC-83. One J-5A Cub Cruiser was evaluated as a small transport but was soon redesignated L-4F. Three others, to have been C-83, were designated L-4F directly. Two J-3Ls to have become UC-83As became L-4C, and one J-4E to have become a UC-83B entered service as an L-4E. The prefix U identified a light C-type with eight or fewer seats.

Royal Air Force Cubs—1940–1943

Britain's Royal Air Force had 26 Cubs in service, but the majority were civil models drafted from private owners (Fig. 5-16). The survivors of these regained their prewar civil registrations after the war and resumed civil operations. Five L-4s were acquired from the U.S. on the Lend-Lease program.

CUB I. British records are contradictory concerning these aircraft. One source shows four Lend-Lease L-4Bs with RAF serials FR886/889 matching U.S. Army serials 43-5137, 5138, 5386, and 5387, but others do not show these RAF serials as having been assigned. Another source lists RAF serials

5-16 The Royal Air Force drafted many civil lightplanes, including 21 Piper J-4A and B Cub Coupes. This J-4A was registered G-AFXS before being drafted as DG 667. It survived the war and was returned to civil use under its original registration.

HK936/939 for the same U.S. serials, apparently a reassignment. One other L-4B, 43-630, received RAF serial VM286.

Unconventional operations

In addition to their normal L-plane operations, the U.S. military Cubs were operated in unconventional ways and assigned missions undreamed of by their designers.

Cubs at sea

On November 9, 1942, three L-4As took off from the aircraft carrier U.S.S. RANGER during the invasion of North Africa (Fig. 5-17). They were to support the artillery ashore. Because of a lack of advance notice of their arrival to the troops and the absence of the L-4 from the current aircraft recognition manual, two were shot down by American ground fire and one by the French, fortunately without fatalities.

Baby carriers

In June 1943, two baby aircraft carriers were developed specifically for the L-4s by modifying LSTs (Landing Ship, Tank) at Bone, Tunisia. A raised runway 16 feet wide and 270 feet long was built down the center of the LST for takeoff

5-17 The first of three L-4As, 42-36389, piloted by Captain Ford E. Allcorn, taking off from the U.S.S. RANGER during the invasion of North Africa, November 9, 1942. The yellow ring painted around the fuselage and underwing insignia was a special application for the invasion.

(Fig. 5-18). Four of the 10 L-4s carried were parked nose-down—2 on either side of the runway—with rudders removed to provide clearance for the L-4s taking off. The other six were on the full-width deck aft of the runway. The L-4s were not expected to land back aboard. One of the baby carriers was used in the invasion of Sicily early in 1943, where the L-4s directed artillery fire that stopped a counterattack by German tanks. Both carriers were used in the landing at Salerno, Italy, in September.

The Brodie Device

To enable L-planes to operate in areas where no suitable landing sites were available, the army adopted a system known as the Brodie Device. Taking an idea tried by the French in 1911, U.S. Army Captain Jeff Brodie developed the system consisting of an overhead cable stretched between two high poles on the ground or between booms swung overside from a ship. A hook-on device on top of the airplane (Fig. 5-19) engaged the cable; the pilot could both take off from the cable and hook back onto it (Fig. 5-20). The Brodie Device was manufactured by All-American Aviation of Wilmington, Delaware, and after the war was approved on ATC A-691 for civil use on the J-3C-65 Cub.

U.S. Army Aviation Museum

5-18 In 1943 the U.S. Army converted two navy LSTs to baby aircraft carriers that could launch but not retrieve 10 L-4s.

Offensive Cubs

In addition to their normal unarmed liaison and observation work, some military Cubs were armed in various ways for offensive missions. Mostly, these were field modifications or outright experiments by stateside development organizations.

In addition to L-4 crews shooting pistols and submachine guns out of the open sides of their Cubs, some planes were fitted with fixed armament. Bomb shackles were mounted on the struts of some with adapters that held up to 10 standard hand-grenades that could be released by a cable from the cockpit (Fig. 5-21). Others mounted six infantry "Bazooka" rocket guns in two three-tube clusters on the struts. One such L-4 is credited with the destruction of five German tanks.

One pure experiment that did not get very far was "Glimpy," a navy NE-1 with a standard navy depth bomb installed in the cockpit (Fig. 5-22). This airplane was controlled by radio from the blimp under which the pilotless Cub was suspended (Fig. 5-23). The odd name was a combination of glider and blimp. The idea was to enable a blimp, which could not maneuver quickly enough, to bomb a surfaced submarine to one side of or behind it, or to attack with a controlled gliding (or even powered) bomb.

5-19 An L-4H, 43-29352, fitted with the Brodie Device that enables the plane to take off from or "land" on an overhead steel cable.

5-20 An L-4H 43-29392 engages the carriage of the Brodie Device rigged over the side of a U.S. Navy ship. Note no-wind condition indicated by the limp flag.

Richard E. Smith

5-21 This L-4B carries 10 standard hand grenades on a makeshift bomb rack on the right wing struts. Pulling a cable in the cockpit releases and arms the grenades.

Postwar L-4s

After V-J Day, most of the L-4 inventory was declared surplus and sold by the War Assets Administration to civil owners. The established price complete was $750. U.S. military authorities in Europe sold over 1000 L-4s over there. Most of the J-3 Cubs on European civil registers today are ex-USAAF L-4s.

In the states, the civilianized L-4s and TG-8s joined the growing J-3 fleet. Many L-4s were retained by the army, however, and some passed to the new U.S. Air Force that was created in September 1947. Others were assigned to Civil Air Patrol (CAP) squadrons where some served in army or air force colors and markings while others acquired civil registrations. The L-4s in postwar military service reflected the practice started in 1944 of painting army/air force airplanes over-all silver.

Late in 1945 a new "buzz number" marking system was adopted for army/air force airplanes to provide easy identification of planes involved in illegal low-flying, or "buzzing." Each aircraft type got a letter, P-for-Pursuit, L-for-Liaison, etc. A second letter identified the model within the type, as LC for the L-4, LD for the Stinson L-5, etc. These were followed by the last three digits of the army/air force serial number, as LC-375 for L-4K 43-1375 (Fig. 5-24).

The few army L-4s used in the Korean War went back into O.D. camouflage

5-22 A radio-controlled U.S. Navy NE-1, 26328, with a depth bomb installed in the cabin.

(Fig. 5-25) to reprise their particular WWII type of operation. Instead of having gray undersides, however, they were olive drab all over. Some silver L-4s merely had O.D. patches applied over their top and side surfaces (Fig. 5-26).

The Flitfires

One batch of 49 J-3s built in 1941 had all the appearance of military airplanes but were not. These were the all-silver "Flitfires," which had a charitable origin.

As a donation to the Royal Air Force Benevolent Fund, to be offered as a prize for a fund-raising drive, William Piper had one J-3F-65, C/N 6600, completed in all-silver finish. This carried RAF military markings, and the special civil registration number NC1776. Franklin donated the engine.

Piper public relations and sales people carried the idea further, and persuaded one Piper dealer in each state to buy a similarly-marked J-3 (Fig. 5-27) with the name of the state painted on the nose, to be flown there in a further fund-raising effort and then to New York City as part of a massive fly-in to further publicize the fund. After a gala banquet attended by the British Ambassador, the owners flew them home, still with their distinctive markings.

5-23 "Glimpy" in launch position under a blimp. A superstructure attached to the blimp ahead of the car contains the radio control equipment and its operator. Initial test flights were made under power with a pilot aboard "Glimpy."

Of the 49 "Flitfires" built, with an approximately equal mix of Continental, Lycoming, and Franklin engines, 15 are still known to be flying. Only one at this writing is painted as a "Flitfire," however.

Wartime restrictions

After Pearl Harbor, CPTP operations carried on briefly in the West Coast defense zone, with special markings applied to the airplanes. These consisted of the large letters U.S. on each side of the fuselage and the U.S. military star-in-circle insignia on the upper left wing and on the lower right wing (opposite locations to the registration numbers, see Fig. 5-28).

Within weeks, however, all civilian school and private operations had to move inland a distance of 150 miles. Planes remaining in the defense zone had to be deactivated by having their propellers and rudders removed.

William T. Larkins

5-24 This L-4K, converted from L-4B 43-1375 after the war, displays the "buzz numbers" adopted for U.S. Army (and later U.S. Air Force) planes in 1945. L identifies a Liaison plane, C the L-4 series, and the numbers are the last three digits of the army serial number.

U.S. Army

5-25 An L-4 with over-all olive drab camouflage lands on a road during the Korean War. Note the long whip antenna for the latter-day radio.

5-26 When L-4J 45-5882 went to Korea it carried standard over-all silver finish. It was soon turned over to the Korean Air Force. The tail number and fuselage buzz number were painted out during the application of blotches of olive drab, but the underwing buzz number LC-882 was retained.

5-27 One of the specially-marked silver J-3 "Flitfires" used to publicize the Royal Air Force benevolent fund, photographed on Oakland Airport, California, on September 24, 1941.

5-28 Immediately after Pearl Harbor, December 7, 1941, privately owned airplanes in the Western Defense Zone were required to carry the letters "U.S." on the fuselage and the military star insignia on the upper left and lower right wing surface. The rudder of this J-3C-50 was reinstalled specifically for this photo, taken January 1, 1942.

6

Postwar boom and bust
Old and new models

As soon as a return to civil airplane production was allowed late in 1945, the principal builders of prewar lightplanes resumed production of their prewar models almost without change. Piper started postwar production with the J-3 and developed two new models, the PA-11 and PA-12, from prewar designs. In 1948 the PA-14 evolved from the PA-12.

Boom

Business boomed for everybody for a while, and even the release of war-surplus equivalents of the Pipers, Taylorcrafts, and Aeroncas at near-junk prices seemed to have no affect on the flood of factory-new lightplanes (Fig. 6-1). Piper, by far the leader in the movement, produced a total of 7773 civil lightplanes in 1946 in spite of a disastrous Lock Haven flood that destroyed many unfinished airplanes and extensive supplies of instruments and materials. Piper eagerly publicized milestones of production (Figs. 6-2, 6-3).

Demand for Piper products was so great that a new factory was set up at Ponca City, Oklahoma, to provide additional manufacturing capability, and Cub Aircraft in Canada built a specialized version of the J-3 there. Piper also built a number of experimental prototypes aimed at the civil market, but none of these airplanes reached production. Demand for the old J-3 and the new PA-11 and PA-12 provided all the business that Piper could handle.

6-1 J-3 Cub production line at Lock Haven in 1946. Note the progressive odd registration numbers on the Cubs facing away from the camera. Those facing the camera have the intervening even registrations.

6-2 Piper eagerly publicized milestone airplanes as shown by this flight view of the 1000th Cub delivered since V-J Day (August 14, 1945). Note wider skylight of postwar J-3.

6-3 Another milestone, the 20,000th Cub, a PA-12 with Piper's second use of the registration number NC20000, posed with E-2 NC15336, C/N 254.

Collapse

Postwar lightplane production soon saturated the existing domestic and export market and sales fell almost to zero by early 1947. By March, the industry had virtually collapsed, with many manufacturers closing their doors forever. Piper, whose payroll was 2607 in February, began cutting back in April. Two-thirds were cut by June, and the Ponca City plant was closed. New York bankers that now controlled the company ceased production at the Lock Haven plant in July but continued an effort to sell on-hand airplanes and unload as much of the materials inventory as possible. By year's end, the payroll was 157.

Recovery

Following a major management shakeup forced by the bankers, the Lock Haven plant reopened to build and sell a new model, the Piper PA-15 "Vagabond," a bare-bones side-by-side two-seater with a 65-hp Lycoming O-145, shortened J-3 wings, and the rest of the airframe built from on-hand materials. The J-3 was dropped from the Piper product line, but sales of the PA-11 and 12 continued and the PA-14 was certificated and put into production.

The postwar J-3 Cub. Outwardly, the postwar J-3 Cub was virtually identical to the 1941 J-3C-65 model: yellow paint, lightning streak, Teddy Bear logo on the tail, and all. Structural improvements were the metal wing spars, the one-piece windshield of the L-4H, a wider skylight like that of the O-59, and a neater carburetor air filter than that of the L-4H (Fig. 6-4). The wingtip bows remained wood, however, and would remain so for all subsequent Cub

6-4 Close-up of a 1946 J-3C-65 shows the main external differences from the prewar J-3: a one-piece windshield and a carburetor air filter that slopes with the cowling instead of projecting forward of it as on the wartime L-4H.

models through the PA-18 Super Cub. The J-3 was still the bare-minimum airplane, however, devoid of an electrical system, and sold for $2195.

In addition to these changes, which are not discernible at a distance, postwar J-3s can be identified by five-digit registration numbers above 42050 or by four-digit numbers followed by a suffix letter.

Fly-away delivery of J-3s was a great opportunity for low-time commercial pilots and Piper employees who wanted to build up their hours and experience for free, plus expenses. Such pilots eagerly came from as far as the West Coast (Fig. 6-5).

Only the J-3C-65 was produced, the more powerful C-85 and C-90 engines added to ATC A-691 were not production installations.

Gross weight was the same 1220 pounds, and the C/Ns continued the prewar J-3 and wartime L-4 C/N series. C/Ns for the 1190 J-3s built at Ponca City started at 21991. This left a gap of 912 C/Ns from the last one assigned to a Lock Haven J-3.

The last of 20,205 J-3s, including their Canadian and military variants, was C/N 23180, NC78439, rolled out at Ponca City on March 4, 1947.

The Cub Prospector. After the war, Cub Aircraft, the Piper subsidiary in Canada, undertook the manufacture of J-3C-65s adapted to Canadian conditions. Seventeen of these were special variants equipped for Canadian bush

6-5 Pilots ferrying J-3 Cubs from the factory to distant destinations did not always refuel at established airports. The Continental A-65 engine could operate just as well on regular auto gas as on the specified 73-octane aviation gas.

flying and winter operations. These were called the L-4B "Cub Prospector" (Fig. 6-6). The rear seat was removable to make room for cargo, the baggage compartment was enlarged, and a 9-gallon auxiliary fuel tank was installed at the rear of the cabin.

6-6 A total of 17 of the 150 J-3s built in Canada after the war were modified for bush flying and were marketed as the L-4B "Cub Prospector."

The Canadian-built J-3s and Prospectors were given a new C/N series, 101C through 250C for the 150 examples built from 1946 into 1952. Color was Tennessee red and Diana cream in the pattern used on the contemporary PA-12 Super Cruiser.

Canadian J-3s and Prospectors were the last Cubs in production to use the famous teddy bear trademark on the tail. The script lettering "Prospector" appeared beneath it when applicable. Canadian registrations for the Prospectors were CF-EEG, EGG/EGU, and EGV.

The PA-11 Cub Special. This major upgrade of the J-3C-65 Cub was marketed as the "Cub Special." The most noticeable change was a closed cowling for the 65-hp A-65-8 engine. Other and more significant changes were internal. An 18-gallon tank in the left wing replaced the 12-gallon nose tank of the J-3. This change allowed the front-seat occupant to sit higher and farther forward. Because of this, the PA-11 could be soloed from the front seat (Fig. 6-7).

6-7 Because of structural and equipment changes, the PA-11 could be soloed from the front seat.

Differences between the J-3 and the PA-11 were far more extensive than those between the J-2 and the J-3. However, the FAA licensed the PA-11 under the old J-3C ATC A-691, and allowed a change to the 90-hp Continental C-90-8F engine that powered the majority of the PA-11s. The fuel-injected 85-hp Continental C-85-8FJ engine and the 100-hp Lycoming O-235-C were also approved for the PA-11 but were not production installations. When the O-235 was installed, the FAA required either 11 pounds of ballast in the rear fuselage or a placard limiting solo flight from the rear seat only.

First flight of the PA-11 was on August 14, 1946, and started a new C/N series at 11-1. The PA-11 was added to ATC A-691 on April 30, 1947, after production was well underway. Gross weight of the 65-hp PA-11 was the same 1220 pounds as the late J-3C-65. Initial color was over-all cub yellow, a straight fuselage stripe with no lightning symbol in front, and no teddy bear on the tail. In place of the teddy bear was the script lettering: "Cub Special." Later, a new Piper Blue and Sport Yellow color scheme was adopted as the PA-11 standard (Fig. 6-8). Price of the 65-hp PA-11 was $2395.

6-8 Coloring of most PA-11s was Piper Blue and Sport Yellow.

Although a few small manufacturers built new airplanes specifically for dusting and spraying, no major manufacturer offered agricultural variants of standard models. Piper became the first to sell factory-equipped agricultural models by fitting removable spray booms and a belly tank to the 90-hp PA-11 (Fig. 6-9).

Piper

6-9 Factory installation of spray booms, chemical tank, and wind-driven pump on an agricultural PA-11. No changes made to cabin; plane can be reconverted easily to standard configuration.

Both the Lock Haven and Ponca City plants built PA-11s, with the latter building 325 of the 1428 civil PA-11 total. Production at Ponca City ended in January 1948 and at Lock Haven in September 1949.

Military PA-11. The U.S. Air Force got interested in a militarized version of the PA-11 to be supplied to other countries under the Mutual Defense Assistance Pact (MDAP). As a result, the last 105 PA-11s were fitted with modified L-4J glasswork and purchased by the air force as L-18Bs. There were no plain L-18s or L-18As.

All of the L-18Bs went to Turkey, and some served that country's forces in the Korean War (Fig. 6-10).

The PA-12 Super Cruiser. In spite of its higher Piper model number, the PA-12 (Fig. 6-11) was in production well before the PA-11. It was a relatively minor refinement of the 1942 J-5C Cruiser, with some details inherited from the HE-1/AE-1, but received a new ATC, A-380. A new C/N series started at 12-1.

The Super Cruiser made its first flight on October 29, 1945, using a modified J-5C, C/N 5-1601, NX41561, as the prototype. The C/N was soon

6-10 One of 105 militarized PA-11s delivered to Turkey as L-18Bs. This one was photographed in Korea during the Korean War. The rear-seat glasswork is slightly shorter than on the WWII U.S. Army O-59A/L-4A and on.

6-11 The 1946 PA-11 Cub Super Cruiser was essentially the 1942 J-5C upgraded for postwar production. The words Piper Cub Super Cruiser appear in very small letters on the fin.

changed to 12-1. Initial powerplant was the 100 hp Lycoming O-235-C, but the O-235-C1, 115 hp for takeoff and 108 hp normal, also was available. The 38-gallon fuel capacity was divided between two 19-gallon tanks, one in either wing. Gross weight was 1750 pounds normal with 1838 maximum, and the price varied from $3295 to $3495.

Standard PA-12 coloring was a Tennessee red wing and horizontal tail and Diana cream fuselage and tail with red fuselage trim in the pattern used on the blue and yellow PA-11s. Again, the teddy bear logo was not used; only the script words "Super Cruiser" below a smaller block-lettered Piper Cub.

Total PA-12 production was 3758. Of these, 236 were built at Ponca City. Surprisingly, 1453 PA-12s were sold in 1946 but ATC A-780 was not issued until March 24, 1947.

Several propeller options were available. The originals were wooden fixed-pitch, but several different fixed-pitch metal models were authorized. A step up in Piper equipment came with the installation of the automatic two-position Koppers Aeromatic propeller that changed pitch automatically as air loads changed.

One crew comfort feature of the PA-12 that proved to be a problem was the pneumatic seat cushions. As the PA-12 got to several thousand feet of altitude, tall occupants found their heads contacting the cabin ceiling as the cushions expanded because of the lower ambient air pressure.

The Super Cruiser was simply a good and reliable three-place airplane. The only notable performance was by a two-plane 22,500-mile flight around the world accomplished by George Truman and Clifford Evans between August 9 and December 10, 1947 (Fig. 6-12).

The last PA-12, C/N 12-4036, N78846, was completed on March 18, 1947, but sales were slow. While 2158 were sold that year, out of a total of 3758 built, only 146 were sold in 1948. A single hangar queen finally sold in 1949.

PA-14 Family Cruiser. As with many aircraft manufacturers, Piper was reluctant to use 13 as model number. The four-place model that followed the PA-12, the "Family Cruiser," therefore became Piper model PA-14.

The Family Cruiser was essentially the Super Cruiser with the forward fuselage widened to allow side-by-side seating in front at dual controls (Fig. 6-13). Powerplant was the Lycoming O-235-C1, delivering 115 hp at 2800 rpm. An innovation for a Piper civil design was the use of wing flaps, the first in production since the L-14. Gross weight of the PA-14 was 1850 pounds. An entirely new color scheme was adopted, with the tail lettering reading "Family Cruiser," as well as a new C/N series starting at 14-1.

The first flight of the Family Cruiser was made on March 21, 1947, but development of the new model was not pushed. A second prototype was

6-12 One of the two Around-the-World Super Cruisers after its return, displaying flags and emblems of all the countries it visited.

6-13 The PA-14 Family Cruiser of 1948 was a four-seat development of the three-place PA-12. Note the addition of wing flaps and the use of a two-position Koppers Aeromatic propeller.

not flown until February 1948, and a new ATC, A-797, was awarded on August 26, 1948.

The Family Cruiser was a victim of bad timing, offered after the collapse of the light airplane boom and not certificated until after closure of the Piper factory. The price was $3825 to $3925. The last Family Cruiser, N5408H, C/N 14-523, was completed on September 9, 1949, but not sold until 1952. Ordinarily, the C/N 14-523 would indicate that 523 PA-14s had been built. Not so; only 238 were built. There was a large gap in C/Ns between 14-204 and 14-490.

The N in the registration reflected a change. In 1948 the second letter of civil registrations was deleted. The N now identified any U.S. registered aircraft. Previously, the second letter identified the type of license—NC for commercial (standard category), NX identified experimental, and NR identified restricted. Experimental and restricted licenses are now identified by the appropriate word in prominent letters on placards near the cockpit or cabin door.

In 1949 Piper got in competition with itself in the four-place, high-wing monoplane field. In December 1948, Piper acquired the Stinson Airplane division of Consolidated-Vultee on a stock trade. Along with the Stinson plant in Wayne, Michigan, came some 200 Stinson 108-3 "Station Wagons," other incomplete airframes, and much material. Although heavier and having 165-hp Franklin engines, the Piper-Stinsons, as they were called, were in direct competition with the Family Cruiser.

7

The Super Cubs

The 90-hp PA-11 Cub Special lifted the Piper Cub out of its traditional role as a bottom-of-the-line primary trainer and greatly expanded its field of activity into just about every line of work that a small airplane could handle. Still more power and the addition of flaps made the excellent short-takeoff-and-landing (STOL) performance of the Cub downright spectacular (Fig. 7-1) and earned it the nickname "the poor man's helicopter." Thanks to its versatility, the PA-18 Super Cub has been in production from 1949 into 1993

The original PA-18 Super Cub, introduced in November 1949, was indistinguishable externally from the PA-11 except for its PA-12/PA-14 rounded rudder, but the structure was considerably strengthened in anticipation of heavier engines and more equipment. The Super Cub was offered in three versions—the bare minimum standard model; the deluxe, with starter, battery, generator, sensitive altimeter, propeller spinner, and other extras; and an agricultural model. A new ATC, 1A-2, was awarded on November 18, 1949, and a new C/N series started with 18-1. Previously, ATCs were issued in numerical order from FAA headquarters in Washington, D.C. Starting in 1948 the system was changed and new ATCs were issued by numbered FAA regions throughout the country. The Certificate number 1A-2 identified the second airplane (A for airplane) approved in FAA Region 1. A second new glider would have been 1G-2 (G for Glider).

The Super Cub also acquired a new Piper logo to replace the famous teddy bear on the tail. This was sort of a compass rose arrangement with the vertical and horizontal words Piper crossing in the middle. Gone, too, was the famous Cub-yellow color scheme. Piper now followed the other airplane manufacturers in the automotive practice of new colors and striping arrangements on a yearly basis.

7-1 The PA-18A-125 was the first of the specialized agricultural Super Cubs. Here a duster demonstrates a steep takeoff after only a 200-foot run.

Production of the Super Cub was entirely at Lock Haven until Piper closed that plant in 1983. After a five-year hiatus, production of the Super Cub was resumed at Piper's plant in Vero Beach, Florida, which was then under new ownership. Super Cub production in the United States was to have ended with the delivery of C/N 1809058 on May 22, 1992. This was the only Super Cub, among several other Piper models, authorized for 1992 production by the bankruptcy court that has controlled Piper since July 1991.

To this point, civil Super Cub production has totalled 8501, exceeding that of the postwar J-3.

The standard-license Super Cub series—1949–1992

All civil Super Cubs except the restricted-license PA-18A (see page 90) were built as PA-18s on ATC 1A-2 regardless of a wide range of horsepower. The only distinctions were dash numbers to the PA-18 designation to indicate the horsepower, and in the case of agricultural and special government training variants, the suffix letters A and T.

Gross weights and prices increased over the years of production. Visual identification of Super Cub variants is sometimes difficult, but in some cases Piper printed the designation, as "Super Cub 125," on the engine cowling or at the front of the fuselage stripe.

PA-18-95. First of the Super Cub models, the PA-18-95, was essentially a PA-11 with heavier structure and the same 90-hp Continental C-90-8F (later-12F) engine. A distinguishing detail was the rounded rudder shape of the PA-12 and PA-14. Normal category gross weight was 1500 pounds; 1400 pounds when operating in the utility category. First flight was late in 1949, with certification received in November. Initial price was $3595 and production continued into 1963, the last example being C/N 18-7632.

PA-18-105. A change to the Lycoming O-235-C engine in 1950 (100 hp at 2600 rpm) resulted in the designation PA-18-105. Production was for only one year before larger engines and new features were added. The price of the PA-18-105 was $2995, cheaper than the -95.

PA-18-105 Special. Also called the PA-18T, the PA-18-105 Special was developed as a military-type trainer and was widely used by the Civil Air Patrol (CAP) and some U.S. Army and Air Force flying clubs as well as for some actual military pilot training (Fig. 7-2). The 243s built in 1952 and 1953 were built as a solid block, with civil registration numbers N100T/342T and C/Ns 2214/2456. Engine was the Lycoming O-235-C1, 108 hp at 2600 rpm.

Some changes from Cub standard to meet military requirements were toe brakes, bucket-type seats for parachutes, and minor equipment revisions. A new

7-2 The PA-18-105 Special, or PA-108-105T, was a special militarized Super Cub. Although some were used to train U.S. Air Force pilots, the training was done by civilian contract schools in airplanes that carried civil markings.

aerodynamic feature that would be featured on all subsequent PA-18 variants was an enlarged horizontal tail with aerodynamically balanced elevators.

PA-18-125. The PA-18-125 made a major step upward in Super Cub evolution (Fig. 7-3). The engine was now the Lycoming O-290-D, delivering 125 hp at 2600 rpm. Normal fuel capacity was still at 18 gallons, but another 18-gallon tank for the right wing was an option. Other than increased power, the major change was the addition of wing flaps. The length of the ailerons was not reduced to make more room for the flaps as had been done on the YL-14s. Gross weight was still 1500 pounds, however. The PA-18-125 was added to ATC 1A-2 on October 25, 1950.

Production life of the PA-18-125 was short, from 1950 into 1953. The U.S. Army and Air Force bought PA-18-125s virtually off-the-shelf as YL-21 and L-21A (see Chapter 8).

7-3 Smooth nose cowling bowl and the presence of wing flaps, plus the words "Super Cub 125" in the fuselage stripe, identify the PA-18-125. The words "Piper Super Cub" on the cowling were put on for this Piper publicity photo.

PA-18-135. When fitted with the later Lycoming O-290-D2 engine (135 hp at 2600 rpm), PA-18-125 airframes with both wing tanks became the PA-18-135. The addition of an oil cooler air scoop at the bottom of the nose cowling bowl distinguished the PA-18-135 from the PA-18-125 (Fig. 7-4). Production of the PA-18-135 continued into 1955.

PA-18-150. The final production version of the Super Cub was the PA-

7-4 This PA-18-135, identified by the oil cooler at the bottom of the cowling bowl is about to take off on a double mission. It will tow a glider to a nearby soaring ridge then proceed into the mountains to drop the salt blocks on the wing bomb racks to cattle in summer pasture.

18-150 (Fig. 7-5), added to ATC IA-2 on October 1, 1954. The engine now was the larger Lycoming O-320 (150 hp at 2700 rpm). Further structural revision brought the normal category gross weight to 1750 pounds and 1500 pounds in the utility category.

Prices for the PA-18-150 started at $5975 and climbed at the rate of nearly $1000 per year. In 1970 it was $15,920 and by 1974 it was $27,110. Final 1982 deliveries by Piper were priced at $47,000.

All PA-18s from C/N18-7633 through 18-9015 were PA-18-150s, after which a new C/N series with a 7-digit dash number, starting with 18-7309016, with a few gaps in this series. With the exception of a single PA-18-160, all in the new C/N series were also PA-18-150s.

PA-18-180. Modifications of PA-18-150s involving 180-hp Lycoming O-360 engines originated with operators in Alaska, where takeoff from glaciers at 14,000 feet or more were required. The larger engines were not approved on ATC IA-2 but by Supplemental Type Certificates (STCs) engineered and obtained by the operator. Piper made only one factory installation of the 180-hp Lycoming in a Super Cub, N2597P, C/N 18-8108008, in 1950.

PA-19. The military L-18B was a PA-11 variant, but the L-18C was a PA-18-95 with military features to which Piper initially assigned the designation PA-19. Only three airplanes carried 19-series C/Ns. After that, Piper consid-

7-5 Piper publicity photo shows a PA-18-150 in a farm setting to emphasize the versatility of the Super Cub. Note fuselage stripes, a major departure from earlier Cub coloring practice.

ered them to be PA-18 variants and assigned C/Ns accordingly. The first two (N501H, N5572H) had 105-hp Lycoming O-235C engines and the third (N5417H) had a 95-hp Continental C-90-12F. Production models used the C-90.

A total of 838 L-18Cs were procured by the USAF for the U.S. Army, but 108 of them went to MDAP nations. The FAA licenses L-18Cs on the civil register under ATC 1A-2.

Agricultural Super Cubs

After WWII, several small aircraft manufacturing firms turned out small quantities of factory-built crop dusters and sprayers, called "agplanes." Most of the agricultural fleet, however, was made up of older civil models that had outlived their normal commercial use, plus many war-surplus biplane trainers.

The popularity of older Cubs from the J-3 up for dusting and spraying made Piper decide to market its own agricultural variant of the Super Cub as a standard-license airplane on ATC 1A-2. A great variety of dust/spray modifications, including tanks, hoppers, dust dispensers, and spray booms, had been developed by the operators. Piper surveyed the field and developed what it considered the most versatile single configuration for the market.

Starting with the PA-18-125, the agplane version had the letter "A" added to its model number. The rear seat was removable to make room for a 110-gallon (18 cubic foot) tank for dust or spray (Fig. 7-6), and a hatch installed in the top of the fuselage for filling it (Fig. 7-7). Rudder travel was increased, and the rudder cables rerouted to clear the tank. Special corrosion-proofing was added to the fuselage structure. Piper also developed its own wind-driven agitator assembly that attached to the belly between the landing gear, and installed standardized spray booms and/or dust dispensers (Fig. 7-8), as had been developed on the. PA-11. Many other installations developed by independent organizations were approved by the FAA for installation in basic PA-18s under ATC 1A-2.

Piper agplane variants were produced as the PA-18A-125, -135, and -150. These agplanes operated on standard licenses if the weight and power limitations of ATC 1A-2 were observed, but higher gross weights were allowed under Civil Air Regulations (CAR) Part 8. Higher gross weight versions of the PA-18A-135 and -150 were built and operated under a separate Restricted Type Certificate (see page 90).

Piper discontinued agricultural versions of the PA-18 after the designed-for-the-purpose PA-25 "Pawnee" agplane was introduced in 1960. Altogether, Piper delivered 2650 PA-18A agplanes.

Piper

7-6 Agricultural PA-18A-150 with dust/spray tank in place of the rear seat and baggage compartment. Note fuel sight gauge in left wing root and that magneto switch is below left window instead of above it as in the J-3.

7-7 Agricultural PA-18s have a hatch in top of the fuselage for filling the hopper. Note the new Piper logo on the fin.

7-8 A PA-18A-150 duster flown on Restricted Type Certificate AR-7. Note the ram-air vent on top of the fuselage, the added access panel on the side, and the RESTRICTED placard in the window.

Restricted-license Super Cubs

A separate type certificate in the restricted category, AR-7, was issued to factory-built PA-18A variants that were to be operated at weights above those permitted by ATC 1A-2. This applied to PA-18A-125s, -135s, and -150s.

The airplanes were classified as single-seaters (1 PCLM for one-place cabin land monoplane) and were authorized to operate at a gross weight of 2070 pounds. The PA-18A-125 was approved on February 5, 1952, the -135 on June 17, 1952, and the -150 on October 7, 1954.

It should be noted that a restricted license does more than merely allow a higher gross weight; there are restrictions on where the airplane can be used, on the economics of the operations, and on the pilot's qualifications.

Restricted-license PA-18As could be converted to standard-license models with kits and instructions provided by Piper.

Military
Super Cubs

After the U.S. Army and Air Force bought militarized PA-11s as L-18B, they acquired militarized Super Cubs as soon as they were available. Some went to U.S. Forces but others were given to MDAP nations. Some small nations not receiving U.S. military Cubs under MDAP acquired civil PA-18s for their military or governmental use on their own.

U.S. military Super Cubs

L-18C. The U.S. Air Force ordered a total of 839 PA-18-95s under the designation of L-18C. Of these, 108 were supplied to MDAP nations. Procurement extended from 1950 through 1953. A single added example was ordered in 1955 for experimental use by the U.S. Army. Oddly, USAF records show that this was procured as a PA-18, but photos show it carrying the L-18C designation (Fig. 8-1).

YL-21. Two PA-18-135s were ordered in 1950 for evaluation under the service test designation of YL-21. After test for suitability as a type, which resulted in production orders, the YL-21s were used to test such new features as rough-terrain landing gear (Fig. 8-2) and for aerodynamic research (see Chapter 10).

L-21A. After test of the YL-21s, the army and air force ordered 150 lower-powered PA-18-125s with a gross weight of 1500 pounds as L-21A. These were ordered in a single block, but the first 30 were essentially off-the-shelf civil models fitted with the 125-hp military O-290-11 engine. These could be distinguished from the other L-21As on the order by their use of civil Super Cub rear windows instead of the military rear-seat glasswork of the

8-1 Although the L-18Cs were Piper PA-18-95s, the army ordered this single PA-18-150 as L-18C 55-4749. Note the X-prefix to the tail number, the word EXPERIMENTAL under the civil PA-18 windows, the controllable-pitch propeller, and the Whittaker tandem landing gear.

8-2 The second of two YL-21s, 51-16496, with silver finish and Whittaker landing gear. The A of the number A-496 on the right wing (last three digits of the serial number and repeated under the left wing) was used for a while to distinguish U.S. Army airplanes from those of the U.S. Air Force.

L-18C (Fig. 8-3). The other L-21As had the L-18 and YL-21 glasswork on the sides (Fig. 8-4) but some did not have the extended transparent cabin roof of the YL-21 (Fig. 8-5). FAA licensed the L-21A as a PA-18-125 on ATC 1A-2.

TL-21A. The T-for-Trainer prefix was added to an unspecified number of L-21As that were modified for use as trainers.

James A. Ruotsala

8-3 The 18th L-21A, 51-15671, with over-all yellow coloring and civil PA-18 rear windows. Note the height of the whip antenna behind the wing and that only the last five digits of the serial number appear on the tail.

L-21B. The 584 L-21Bs were PA-18-135s with civil Lycoming O-290-D2 engines, glasswork as most L-21As and the L-18s, and a gross weight of 1760 pounds. Again, many were sent to MDAP nations (Fig. 8-6). FAA licensed the L-21B as a PA-18-135 on ATC 1A-2.

U-7A. Redesignation of some U.S. military aircraft in 1962 resulted in L-21Bs still in service being redesignated U-7A in the new U-for-Utility category.

Foreign military Super Cubs

Exact figures are not available on the distribution of L-21s to MDAP nations, but they are known to have been used by at least the following:

Austria   PA-18
Belgium   Six L-18C used as target tugs in 1969

Denmark	L-18C
Germany	L-18C
Ghana	PA-18-150
Greece	L-18C
Italy	20 L-18C and 62 L-21B
Japan	47 L-21B (Fig. 8-6)
Luxembourg	L-18C
Netherlands	L-21A
Norway	L-18C
Nicaragua	3 PA-18
Portugal	PA-18-125
Sweden	12 L-18C
Switzerland	PA-18-125
Uganda	18 civil PA-18s for government/military use
Uruguay	2 L-18C

Dustin W. Carter

8-4 A late L-21A, with full tail number 115800, over-all yellow finish, and transparent cabin roof. Note the fixed-pitch metal propeller with 125-hp Lycoming O-290-11 engine.

Civil-registered military Super Cubs

In the U.S. the Civil Air Patrol (CAP), some U.S. Army and Air Force flying clubs, and civil contract flying schools giving instruction to the military, used

Piper via Roger Peperell

8-5 The 32nd L-21A, 51-15695, with silver finish and L-18 type rear windows but with less transparent top to the cabin than on the YL-21s.

Norman E. Taylor

8-6 The 135-hp L-21B could be distinguished from the 125-hp L-21A by the oil cooler at the bottom of the nose bowl. This camouflaged example in the Swedish Army also has an external air filter for the carburetor air intake.

PA-18-105 Specials (PA-18Ts) with civil registrations rather than military designations and serial numbers. Some of these carried nonstandard "buzz numbers" (see page 64) on their fuselages with the letters TA and the last three numbers of the civil registration (Fig. 8-7). In the regular "buzz number" system TA identified the North American T-6 "Texan" trainer, formerly AT-6.

8-7 A yellow PA-18T with unfaired landing gear, Civil Air Patrol insignia under the rear window, and U.S. Air Force Training Command insignia under the windshield. The word COLUMBUS above that insignia means that the plane was based at Columbus, Mississippi. The 275 in the unofficial buzz number TA-275 is the last three digits of the civil registration N275T, visible in 2-inch figures on the rudder.

9

Cubs on
floats and skis

As with most conventional airplanes, the utility of the Cub from the J-2 on could be increased by fitting it with twin pontoons, commonly called floats, or with skis. Although mostly used on civil models, the U.S. Army and Navy used Cubs on floats and skis during WWII and later (Figs. 9-1 and 9-2).

Cub seaplanes

When a Cub is operated as a seaplane, the letter S is added to the Taylor or Piper model number, as J-2S, PA-18-125S, etc.

Normal procedure in converting a landplane to a seaplane is to remove the landing gear, add attachment fittings to the lower longerons for the float struts, and install the floats and their rigging. A net weight increase reduces the useful load of the airplane since the landplane gross weight is not usually exceeded. Cruising speed drops for two reasons. First, increased drag of the floats slows the plane. Second, the propeller pitch is reduced on seaplanes to get maximum engine revolutions at a lower airspeed than on an equivalent landplane.

Most, but not all, Cubs were approved for floats. In the U.S. these floats were mostly the all-metal Edo (acronym for Earl D. Osborn, the builder) of College Point, New York. Some foreign-owned Cubs used floats from other builders (Fig. 9-3) and some wooden substitutes were built in the U.S. during WWII.

The numbers associated with float designs identify the pounds of water displaced by one completely submerged float. Since approximately a 100

9-1 A USAF L-4J assigned to the Civil Air Patrol in 1949 is outwardly identical to the civil J-3C-65 on Edo 1320 floats. The single water rudder on left float was standard installation.

9-2 L-4J 44-80091 on skis during the Battle of the Bulge, December 1944. Remnants of July invasion stripes remain on lower sides and bottom of fuselage.

9-3 A surplus L-4J in Norwegian civil markings displays a nonstandard method of float attachment. The forward float fitting attaches to the standard landplane landing gear.

percent reserve of buoyancy is required for approval, the displacement number of a single float will equal or slightly exceed the gross weight of the airplane. The early J-3, using Edo D-1070 floats, had a gross weight of 1070 pounds.

Seaplane operations introduced special problems for some Cubs in addition to normal floatplane differences. On Cubs, and other airplanes without starters, the pilot or passenger had to stand on the right float and swing the propeller from behind (Fig. 9-4). This starting procedure is not difficult on low-powered airplanes like Cubs.

Sometimes it is hard to get a loaded low-powered airplane like a J-3C-65S off the water. Pilots then resort to a trick of rolling the plane onto one float, once planing speed is reached, to reduce water drag and pick up the few extra mph needed to get into the air (Fig. 9-5).

Float models and sizes for approved U.S. Cub seaplanes are listed by Cub model.

E-2. The E-2 never appeared as a seaplane but was approved for four different makes of skis.

F-2. One F-2, X14729, C/N 115, was tested on Edo model 990 floats, the smallest that Edo built, but was not approved (Fig. 9-6).

Norm Petersen

9-4 Hand-propping a Cub seaplane has to be done from behind the propeller while standing on the right-hand float. The plane is Norm Petersen's J-3C-65 fitted with a 90-hp Continental C-90.

This plane is an excellent example of an upgraded rather than a pure antique. A Taylor J-2 Cub, NC16769, C/N 771, it has a postwar J-3 Cub's one-piece windshield and sloping carburetor air filter. Old-style NC numbers are on the tail but not on the wing. Photographed in 1991.

Howard Levy

Norman Petersen

A field of yellow dandelions—weeds and the airplane that proliferated like weeds—the yellow Piper J-3 cub. This J-3C-65 has a special registration number, N10XS, which translates to "One Old Ex-Sprayer." It was a sprayer for 20 years before being restored as a sportplane.

A Canadian-registered Piper PA-18-105S Super Cub raises its right wing to make a one-float takeoff.

Gordon McNulty

A 1946 J-3C-65 with the turtledeck cut down and the cabin structure removed for totally open flying. Although it is a postwar model, the carburetor air filter has been removed and the exhaust system modified.

This 1939 J-3C, N25749, C/N 3707, was modified after the war for a comedy and daredevil act at air shows on an Experimental-Exhibition license.

This Alaska-based Piper PA-14S Family Cruiser with modified wingtips and tail surfaces carries a kayak tied to the right-side float struts.

A yellow L-18C with added high-visibility markings of the German Luftwaffe. This one is now used for glider towing. Note the rearview mirror on the strut and the tow hitch on the tailwheel bracket.

The first of two Piper YL-21's, 51-6495, in the original silver finish with high-visibility Day-glow red markings for test purposes.

In 1962, after this L-21B, 54-2412, was supplied to Holland under the MDAP program, its designation was changed to U-7B. This photograph was taken June 30, 1973.

A rare Piper Cub J-3P, NC21561, C/N 2474, with the 50-hp Lenape Papoose three-cylinder radial engine.

Bud Blancher

Bud Blancher of Eatonville, Washington, built two special small bicycles for transportation at air shows and other away-from-home locations. He carries them on the struts of his J-3C-65 Cub in an FAA-approved installation.

Two notably different three-cylinder radial engines were used in Cubs. The J-3P (top) used the 50-hp Lenape Papoose, which was used in the F-2 under its original name—Aeromarine AR-3. Note the prominent push rods in front of the cylinders. The H-2 used the 35-hp Szekely SR-3 (bottom). Note the cable assembly required by the FAA to keep cracked cast-iron cylinders from blowing off the engine.

Charles N. Trask

Golda Cox

Don Downie

9-5 Slightly exaggerated attitude of a J-3C-65 while demonstrating the one-float takeoff technique. This J-3C-65 has a Super Cub rudder.

Taylor via Howard Levy

9-6 The only early Cub tried on floats was this F-2 with Edo 990 floats.

H-2. No seaplane approval.

J-2. The initial float approval was for Edo model D-1070 floats. When these were used, a small vertical fin had to be added near each tip of the horizontal stabilizer (Fig. 9-7). When the slightly larger Edo 54-1140 floats were used, the extra fin area was not required. The 1070 floats added 68 pounds to the empty weight of the J-2 and $625 to the price.

9-7 An oddity. A J-2S with its floats removed but still retaining the required seaplane tail fins. The rear float strut attachment fitting is just aft of open door.

J-3 (ATC A-660). The J-3 was approved for Edo D-1040 floats, and like the J-2, required extra fin area when using them. If the larger 54-1140 floats were used, extra fins were not required. Some J-3s in other countries, with different design floats, did require added fin area (Fig. 9-8).

J-3C (ATC A-691). Over its long production life and continuing career, the J-3C acquired a greater number of floats than the one for which it was originally certificated, as well as larger floats, as follows:

Capre 1500 ($10,500)
Edo D-1070
Edo 54-1140 (J-3C gross weight 1140 pounds)
Edo 60-1320 (The most widely used after WWII for gross weight of 1300 pounds)

Charles W. Cain

9-8 Another surplus L-4J in Norway, this one with added tail fin. Compare float shape and strut arrangement with standard American struts and Edo 1320 floats.

Edo 92-1400 (J-3C-65 only)
Heath 1460A (J-3C-65 only)
McKinley PF-2 Pneumatic (see page 106) Gross weight 1130 pounds for J-3C-50, 1160 pounds for J-3C-65.
Wollam 1200 - Wooden (see page 106).

J-3F. Gross weight 1160 pounds on the following floats:

Edo 54-1140
Heath 1460A (J-3F-65 only)

J-3L. Gross weight 1160 pounds on the following floats:

Edo 54-1140
Edo 60-1320
Heath 1460A (J-3L-65 only)

J-3P. The J-3P was not approved for floats, but one was used as a test airplane for the unique McKinley PF-2 Pneumatic floats.

J-4 Series. FAA specifications show that only the J-4 and J-4A were approved on Edo 60-1320 floats at 1350 pounds gross weight (Fig. 9-9).

J-5 Series. All approved for Edo 89-2000 floats for an empty weight increase of 183 pounds. Maximum gross weight for J-5C, 1550 pounds.

PA-11. The PA-11 was approved only for Capre 1500, Edo 60-1320, and Edo 92-1400 floats at a gross weight of 1300 pounds. Modification of the engine cooling air flow was required for the PA-11S.

PA-12. Approved for Edo 89-2000 floats and was the first Cub since the

9-9 A Canadian J-4A Cub Coupe on Edo 1320 floats with different fuselage attach points for float struts compared to J-3/L-4.

9-10 Three-place Canadian PA-12 Cub Super Cruiser on Edo 2000 floats. Sunlight shining through stabilizer-elevator gap gives the false impression that the underfin is hinged at the rear.

plain J-3 on ATC A-660 to require additional fin area. This was in the form of a single surface below the rear end of the fuselage (Fig. 9-10).

PA-14. Not approved for floats.

PA-18 Series. Approved on Edo 92-1400 floats for models up to PA-18-135. Models PA-18-125 and up can use 89-2000 floats. The in-between model 88-1650A floats sold for $11,990 in 1983.

Like the J-3, the PA-18 Super Cub used a wide range of floats in different sizes and by different manufacturers. It should be noted that the struts for Super Cub floats hold the fuselage higher above the water than on the J-3 and PA-11 (Fig. 9-11). Approved PA-18 floats:

Canadian Aircraft Products 2000 ($13,536)
Capre 1500 (PA-18-95, -105 only)
Capre 1900 on PA-135, -150 ($12,300)
Edo 92-1400 on PA-18-85 to PA-18-135
Edo 88-1650A ($12,990 in 1983, $19,300 in 1992)
Edo 89-2000 ($20,000 in 1992)
Fiberfloat 2400 (Built of Kevlar; price $13,400)

PA-18A Restricted. Not approved for floats, but some PA-18As on ATC 1A-2 do operate as floatplanes, presumably with the designation PA-18AS.

9-11 In spite of similar-sized airframes, Super Cub seaplanes like this PA-18-135S are farther above the water than the J-3 and PA-11. Note the longer float struts, and water rudders on both Edo 1650 floats.

Pneumatic floats

In 1939 Ashley C. McKinley, operator of a seaplane base, took a new approach to float construction. He formed floats of reinforced rubber and inflated them like balloons to a pressure range of 1.25 to 1.75 pounds per square inch. He got these approved, and some were used on J-3 Cubs (Fig. 9-12).

9-12 Although approved for the J-3 Cub and other lightplanes, the McKinley pneumatic floats of 1939–40 were not notably successful. This pair is being tested for takeoffs and landings on ice.

While they worked well on water at sea level, they expanded as altitude increased. Enough pressure could be built up in high flight to bleed off some air and lower the pressure below the minimums for landing. Needless to say, the McKinley floats were not around for long.

Pneumatic floats are making a comeback in the 1990s. Wag-Aero of Lyons, Wisconsin, and Lotus, Canadian maker of pneumatic floats for ultralight and homebuilt airplanes, have developed a set for Wag-Aero's CubY J-3 replica (see Chapter 12). It is possible that these can be certificated for use on J-3s.

Wooden floats

Just before WWII something new appeared on the market—simple and low-cost wooden floats. Developed by the Wollam firm, these featured slab-sided

9-13 The wooden Wollam floats were an attempt to reduce the high cost of metal floats by using simple wood construction. There is an entirely different strutting arrangement on this J-3C-65 compared to other J-3s on Edo metal floats.

plywood construction instead of more expensive formed metal. Strutting arrangement was entirely different than for the more common Edos (Fig. 9-13). The army and navy used some during the war, and wooden floats were briefly popular on the postwar surplus market.

Amphibious floats

Twin floats containing fixed or retractable wheels were tried even before WWI, but found little use. Interest picked up just before WWII, and Edo developed models with retractable main wheels behind the step and smaller retractable wheels in the bows. With the main wheels behind the airplane's center of gravity, piloting technique is as for tricycle-gear landplanes instead of conventional-gear "taildraggers."

Military needs accelerated development and production during WWII and postwar civil use has been extensive. Quite a few Super Cubs can be seen on Edo amphibious floats today (Fig. 9-14).

9-14 Edo amphibious floats on a PA-18-150 fitted with booster wingtips. The front wheels retract upward and remain outside the floats; the rear wheels retract backward and upward into the float behind the step.

Dry takeoffs and landings

Often, landplanes are put on floats at an airport that is not near water. That problem is solved easily by placing the floatplane level on a three-or-four-wheeled dolly. The plane and dolly are lined up with the runway and the pilot applies takeoff power. The combination rolls down the runway until the plane has enough airspeed to lift off (Fig. 9-15). The dolly rolls on until it stops. Some elaborate dollies that are used frequently have brakes that are applied automatically after the plane lifts off.

The reverse situation, landing a seaplane on the grass alongside a paved runway, is also common practice. It is then relatively easy for three or four people to get a J-3 or a Super Cub onto a dolly and roll it to the hangars. Both the dry landing and the dry takeoff are used frequently as air show acts.

Cub skiplanes

All Cub models were approved for use of skis, far too many individual makes and models to list here. In most cases, the pedestal of the ski is simply fitted on the landing gear axle in place of the wheel (Fig. 9-16). Depending on snow conditions, some skiplanes retain their steerable tailwheels (Fig. 9-17).

Richard H. Wagner

9-15 The prototype Wag-Aero CubY (see Chapter 13), fitted with Full-Lotus pneumatic floats, demonstrates a dry takeoff from a paved runway by means of a three-wheel dolly.

Max Witters Jr.

9-16 Most skis, like these metal Federals, fit easily on the wheel axles, as on this J-3C-65. The brake drums are left on. Rubber cords on front of skis pull them to flight position determined by the length of the rear steel cables.

Horace C. Pearman

9-17 I am checking out on skis in a J-3C-65 Cub, February 1949. Because only a few inches of snow covers a paved runway, the tail wheel has been left on the Cub.

While most skis are aligned with the line of flight by a rubber cord, or bungee, pulling against a rear restraining cable, others use hydraulic snubbers. A late 1930s example is the J-5B Cub Cruiser of Fig. 9-18 fitted with Model A Ford automotive shock absorbers adapted for the job.

Charles N. Trask

9-18 The Marston skis on this J-5B Cub Cruiser use hydraulic snubbers for in-flight positioning instead of the rubber-cord-and-wires arrangement illustrated previously.

Ski-wheels

The utility of the Cub, particularly the hardworking Super Cub, is increased by the use of ski-wheels. On these, the standard wheel projects a short distance through the ski, permitting landings both on snow and on snow-free surfaces (Fig. 9-19).

9-19 This PA-18-125 with J-3/PA-11 rudder is flying on an experimental license while testing Landis combined wheel-ski landing gear. Small "tailwheels" keep the heels of the skis from dragging on the pavement.

Water skis

Alaskan pilots long ago perfected a technique for landing ski-equipped airplanes on smooth water and then maintaining enough forward speed to keep the plane from sinking until it could be run up on a beach or mud flat. Take-off can also be made from a running start on mud or from shallow water parallel to a beach (Fig. 9-20).

9-20 A PA-11S starts a water takeoff from a beach on the water skis developed by the All American Engineering Co. The tail stays up during the water operation so there is no need to remove the tailwheel.

To provide adequate planing area, the skis must be fairly wide, not the narrow metal models that are practically ice skates. The tail does not come down during these water operations, so tail wheels can be left on.

All-American Engineering Co. of Wilmington, Delaware, developed a special set of combined ski-wheels and water skis and tested it on a PA-11 (Fig. 9-21).

9-21 Closeup of the All American water ski and wheel landing gear. Note revised landing gear shock absorbers and the width of the water skis.

10

Modified Cubs

As is inevitable with any major production airplane in service for an appreciable length of time, the Cub acquired an interesting collection of modifications. Some of these, of course, were tests by Piper to try various improvements for the basic design while others simply used the Cub as the test bed for something new that had no direct application to Cub development.

Many modifications have been made by individuals in two separate areas: pure recreation and the desire to tinker with airplanes for amusement; and serious modifications worked out by commercial users to improve the performance, payload, utility, and/or earning power of their Cubs.

In most cases, changes were worked out by the owners/operators without help from or even the knowledge of Piper. Modifications desirable for wider commercial use could be sold to other Cub operators following an FAA approval and the issuance of a Supplemental Type Certificate (STC) in the name of the originator, not Piper.

In some cases, improvements developed by outsiders have been adopted by Piper for subsequent production. An example is the turned-around landing gear developed in 1948 that allowed the J-3 and PA-11 to be converted to a tricycle (Fig. 10-1). Piper didn't put that in production on Cubs, but offered it as an option for the later model PA-20 Pacer, which was redesignated the PA-22 Tri-Pacer. The three-wheel model became so popular that it became the major production model and the PA-20 was discontinued.

Since even brief descriptions of notable Cub modifications would more than fill a book of this size, the selections used in this chapter are limited mainly to captioned photos. These are grouped in areas: Piper's own modifications, recreational modifications, and individuals' modifications intended to increase the utility and revenues of their Cubs.

10-1 Tricycle landing gear for J-3 and PA-11 Cubs consisted of turning the standard landing gear around in the original fittings to put the wheels behind the center of gravity and adding a nose wheel. I flew this one in 1949, my first experience with tricycle landing gear.

Factory modifications

As mentioned in Chapters 2 and 3, Taylor and Piper made state-of-the-art improvements to the basic Cub production models to keep them competitive in the market. Other factory changes were of an experimental nature that were not adopted, such as full span flaps on a J-3 (Fig. 10-2), a variable camber wing on a J-4 test bed (Fig. 10-3), and a full-cantilever wing for the J-3. Some production features, as the rear window for the L-4, were worked out on a J-3 that Piper used as a company test plane. A Taylor experiment tried an increased wing dihedral angle on a J-2 (Fig. 10-4).

Recreational modifications

Some private owners have made relatively minor modifications to their Cubs that do not affect the standard license under which they are flown. These include stripping off the upper rear fuselage superstructure and cabin sides and flying the Cub "open cockpit" (Fig. 10-5).

Others are so extreme that the Cub has to be flown on an experimental license with attendant restrictions and sometimes loses its identity as a Cub. The twin-engine conversion of Fig. 10-6 is an extreme example. Owners are willing to accept the limitations of X-licenses for the satisfaction of having a truly unique airplane.

Piper

10-2 Experimental modification of a J-3C-65 during development of the L-14 wing featured trailing edge flaps, synchronized drooping ailerons, and spoilers added for improved roll control.

After the construction and operation of amateur-built, or homebuilt, airplanes became legal in 1947, some builders used cut-down components of production airplanes as shortcuts to completion of their dream ships (Fig. 10-7). This disturbed manufacturers like Piper, who might see the wing of a 65-hp Cub put on a more powerful design, or subjected to stresses for which it was never designed. If the Piper wing failed in flight, unfavorable publicity would reflect on Piper.

FAA put an end to this practice after a few years by enacting the "51 percent rule," whereby the builder actually had to build 51 percent or more of the airplane himself. Planes built before adoption of the rule could continue to fly, however. Another recreational modification is shown in Fig. 10-8.

Piper via Howard Levy

10-3 A prewar Piper experiment fitted the Rose Slotted Wing to a J-4 Cub Coupe. No further development of this variable-camber wing was undertaken.

Taylor

10-4 A Taylor experiment tried greatly increased wing dihedral on a J-2 Cub. Note the nonstandard merging of the exhaust stacks on each side of the A-40 engine.

10-5 Postwar recreational modification of a J-3C-65 Cub by a private owner. Even the windshield has been deleted for totally open-air flying.

10-6 Although retaining most of its original outline, this J-3C Cub has been converted to a twin-engine plane with 65-hp Lycomings. The owner registered it as the Miller M-6, not a Piper Cub.

10-7 In the early years of legal amateur aircraft construction, builders could use cut-down components of factory-built airplanes. This Nelson N-4 used to be a J-3C-65 Cub.

10-8 With its unique transparent covering, other modifications to this J-3C-65 Cub, such as the clipped wing with squared-off tips, are not so noticeable.

Aerobatics modifications

To improve the aerobatic capability of their Cubs, either for professional air show work or recreational aerobatics, many owners developed clipped-wing Cubs by shortening the wing span to improve the rate of roll. Usually this was done by shortening the wings at the inner ends and shortening the struts, leaving the ailerons full length (Fig. 10-9). Some individuals and firms have obtained STCs for clipped wings so that private owners can modify their Cubs for recreational aerobatics but still retain a standard license. Wings shortened by 12 feet were approved for J-3C Cubs on ATC A-691 before adoption of the STC system.

10-9 Most popular modification of Cubs for increased aerobatic capability is the clipped wing, with six feet taken off the inner end of each wing. Full-size ailerons now extend nearly to the fuselage and original rounded wingtips are retained on this J-3C-65.

Some aerobatic modifications are so extensive, involving shortened fuselages as well as clipped wings and increased power, that the modified airplane loses its Cub identity and acquires a new name (Fig. 10-10). Such modifications put the planes on experimental-exhibition licenses, under which the airplanes can earn money. The experimental amateur built license issued to homebuilts allows recreational use only.

Other air show Cub modifications are shown in Chapter 11. Piper produced only one aerobatic J-3, a clip-wing special for famous air show pilot Beverly "Bevo" Howard in 1941. This used a special fuel-injected Continental C-85 engine, an inverted fuel system, and had a cleaned-up landing gear with enclosed shock absorbers. Howard used NX38335 to win two national aerobatic

10-10 Some aerobatic Cub modifications are so extreme that the plane loses its identity as a Cub. This former J-3C-65 has been renamed the Meyers M-1 by its owner/builder, Pete Meyers.

championships. It then passed to another show pilot, Charles Hillard, who modified it further (Fig. 10-11), then to its present owner, Robert Copeland. Copeland installed clipped Taylorcraft wings with their NACA 23012 airfoil for better inverted flight, and a 180-hp Lycoming engine. Rate of climb is 3000 feet per minute!

10-11 The only factory-built clipped-wing Cub was a special J-3C for air show pilot Bevo Howard in 1941 with old plain ailerons and modified landing gear. This postwar modification is by Charles Hillard, who added closed cowling and more power.

Utility modifications

Many different modifications, from minor to radically major, have been made to Cubs to improve their aerodynamics, load capacity, utility, and earning power. Some of these are discussed in the following paragraphs.

Rough-terrain landing gear

To enable Cubs to operate from terrain too rough for normal airplane operations, individuals have taken different approaches to the problem. One of the first, developed by Art Whittaker of Portland, Oregon, in 1949, was to create a four-wheel "bogie" landing gear. This uses four standard 8.00 x 4.00 wheels, two each on yokes that fit on the standard axle (Fig. 10-12). The rear wheel of each unit is fitted with brakes. The arrangement works well on rough surfaces, but tight turns on the ground are difficult.

10-12 Whittaker tandem landing gear for Cubs operating on rough terrain was approved for all Cubs and equivalent lightplanes and saw fairly wide use from 1949 on. This one is a PA-11-90.

During WWII and shortly afterward, several manufacturers tried track-type landing gear on such large planes as twin-engine attack planes and four-engine bombers. Several individuals tried them on Cubs after the war (Fig. 10-13), but the scheme was not adopted.

10-13 Another approach to rough-terrain landing gear for Cubs was this postwar Italian experiment with tread-type landing gear on a PA-18-135 Super Cub.

The simplest and most popular solution to the rough or soft terrain problem is to fit greatly oversize tires on single wheels to the standard landing gear of a Cub or other airplane (Fig. 10-14). Developed in Canada for use in the tundra, these are called "tundra tires" and are readily available from several commercial sources.

10-14 Simplest solution to operation on rough on or soft ground was to use oversize tires called "tundra tires" like on this Canadian-registered PA-18-150. The bulge on top of the fuselage is an emergency radio transmitter.

Crosswind landing gear

Near the end of WWII experiments were made to develop crosswind landing gear; that is, wheels that could align with the runway while the airplane was crabbed into a strong crosswind during takeoff and landing. Early experiments on an L-4 involved swivelling the entire wheel (Fig. 10-15), but the final configuration had the swivel inside the wheel itself, which was mounted on a standard axle (Fig. 10-16).

All American Aviation

10-15 War-surplus L-4B NX42045 was used to develop the original crosswind landing gear. Here each wheel swivels under a new rigid landing gear truss.

10-16 Final form of the crosswind landing gear with swivelling wheels looks like any normal landing gear. This surplus L-4B carries the low registration NC254.

Wingtip modifications

Various individuals sought to get a bit more performance out of their Cubs by improving the aerodynamics of the wing through wingtip modification. One way was to increase the area slightly by squaring off the wingtip (Fig. 10-17). A variation was to add end plates to a squared-off wingtip (Fig. 10-18). The idea was that the plates would improve airflow by preventing flow of air over the wingtip. The plates accomplished this, but the added drag of the wetted area of the plate itself and the intersection drag on both surfaces of the wing largely offset the advantages of the plates. This modification fell out of favor and is seldom seen today.

10-17 Squared-off wingtips add wing area and supposedly a bit more lift to this PA-11-90 used as a glider tug.

The most effective wingtip modification is the addition of booster tips. These are moulded plastic extensions for the tips that are easy to install. They are scientifically shaped to control the drag-producing wingtip vortices and have a distinctive downward twist (Fig. 10-19). These tips are covered by STCs and can be installed on any standard-licensed Cub.

Agricultural modifications

Many old Cubs that had outlived their normal private or commercial usefulness were converted to crop dusters or sprayers. Some modifications were as simple

10-18 PA-12 Super Cruiser with wingtips modified to take end plates intended to reduce loss of lift due to airflow spilling off of wingtips.

10-19 A PA-18 Super Cub fitted with Booster wingtips and painted as a J-3. Note the aerodynamic fences controlling spanwise air flow and that the N in the tail number N7037H is backward.

as installing the chemical tank in the back seat and adding a dust dispenser or spray booms. Some sprayers added a removable belly tank. Such conversions could be changed back to normal configuration with relative ease. Other modifications have been so extreme that the airplane is hardly recognizable as a Cub and the modifications are hardly reversible. Some of these are shown in Figs.10-20 through 10-24. Some agricultural Cubs in action can be seen in Chapter 12.

10-20 This highly-modified 1941 J-3 was photographed in 1955 while serving as a sprayer. It has a cut-down turtledeck, squared-off wingtips, uncowled engine, and flame-damping exhaust stacks to reduce fire hazard.

10-21 This 1946 J-3C-65 has similar wing and fuselage modifications to Fig. 10-20, but has replaced the engine with a 125-hp Lycoming. What appears to be a lower wing is actually an aid to dusting. Downwash from the added surface, marketed as the Distributor Wing, improves dust distribution.

10-22 A 1946 J-3C-65 extensively modified for spraying. Note spray booms, cowled engine, and cut-down fuselage with open cockpit at the rear seat position.

10-23 A less extreme agricultural modification of a J-3C-65 Cub. This sprayer's entire fuselage is covered with sheet aluminum.

10-24 Resemblance to a Cub in this PA-12 Super Cruiser duster conversion exists only in memory. Fuselage, tail and landing gear have been reshaped, a 220-hp Continental R-670 radial engine replaces the O-235 Lycoming, and a lower wing has been added.

Miscellaneous modifications

Some Cub modifications that do not quite fit the previous categorizations are presented here in decreasing order of magnitude. First is the Wagner Twin Cub, created by Harold Wagner of Portland, Oregon, in 1949 (Figs. 10-25 and 10-26). This used two Cub fuselages, one a PA-11 and one a J-3, placed very close together. The problem of propeller clearance was solved by putting a machined spacer behind the 85-hp Continental engine in the left-hand (PA-11) fuselage. Outer wing panels were standard Cub size. The landing gear was reinforced and short center sections were built between the fuselages for wings and tail. Needless to say, this Twin Cub was a one-only.

Another one-only was an Army YL-21 modified extensively by Mississippi State College for research into air flow and boundary layer control. The wing was sealed and myriad small slots cut in it to permit the boundary layer to be sucked inside the wing by an engine-driven pump in the nose (Fig. 10-27). For some testing, the YL-21 was towed aloft without its propeller to fly as a glider free of the normal turbulent slipstream (Fig. 10-28).

A lesser modification put a new metal-skinned single-spar wing on a PA-12 (Fig. 10-29). Other metalwork approved for PA-12s and added to ATC A-780 was developed in 1954 by the Met-Co-Air Company of Fullerton, California. The company replaced the fabric of the fuselage and fin with sheet aluminum (Fig. 10-30).

10-25 Harold Wagner of Portland, Oregon, joined a PA-11 fuselage (right) to a J-3 fuselage with 85-hp Cowled Continental engine to form the Wagner Twin Cub in 1949. Propeller overlap was made possible by a spacer behind the PA-11's propeller.

10-26 Wagner's joined Cubs retained their original PA-11 and J-3 factory color schemes. Note the added stabilizer and elevator between the two fuselages.

10-27 The second YL-21 was extensively modified for an aerodynamic research program with Cessna-type spring steel main landing gear. Bulge above nose houses a pump that sucks boundary-layer air into the wing.

10-28 The modified YL-21 being flown as a glider. Wool tufts taped to top of wing show changes in airflow over the wing. Note small airflow fences at gap between flaps and ailerons.

10-29 An entirely new single-spar metal-skinned wing was installed on this PA-12 Super Cruiser. Note new wingtip shape and single wing strut.

Chalmers Johnson via Peter Berry

10-30 Met-Co-Air developed a sheet aluminum replacement for the fuselage and fin fabric of the PA-12 Super Cruiser and it was approved on ATC A-780. Note the small added dorsal fin.

Availability and simplicity of the Cub made it a natural test-bed for new small engines, and several in the U.S. and Europe were used for this purpose (Fig. 10-31). However, the modified J-3 shown in Fig. 10-32 was not trying a new engine. Propeller maker Ole Fahlin of Sunnyvale, California, installed an antique 90-hp British Pobjoy radial in his modified J-3 for his own amusement. The engine was geared down so far that a large-diameter, large-area propeller was required, so Fahlin crafted the special three-blade design.

10-31 A twin-engine J-3 with a different purpose. This airplane was modified by Nelson Aircraft Corp. of Irwin, Pennsylvania, to serve as a test bed for the 37-hp Nelson H-63 two-cycle engine. N6411H is 139 pounds lighter than a standard J-3C-65 and can climb at 1500 feet per minute.

10-32 Owner Ole Fahlin installed this antique 90-hp British Pobjoy radial engine for his own amusement and accepted the limitations of an experimental license. Large-area propeller required by extensive gearing-down of the engine.

One very unusual modification approved for the J-3C-65 on ATC A-691 is an arrester gear to stop the plane in a short distance. This was developed by All-American Aviation, Inc. during WWII. The system uses an explosive charge in a "gun" in the fuselage to drive a spike into the ground (Fig. 10-33). A cable woven from Unolyn, a fiber that can be stretched to three times its original length, is attached to the plane and to the spike. The stretching of the Unolyn absorbs the energy of the deceleration.

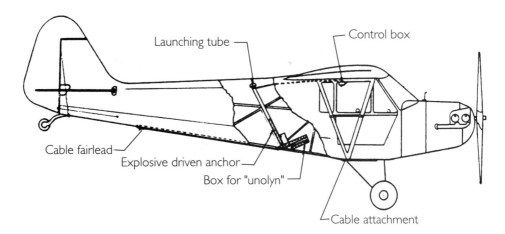

10-33 Cutaway drawing shows the installation of the All American Aviation arrester equipment in a J-3. With the Cub's known short-field capability, such an installation was hardly worth the cost and effort. All American Aviation.

This system has stopped a J-3 in a distance of 100 feet but is rough on the plane. After an arrested landing the plane is grounded until a thorough inspection is made and signed off in the logbook.

Another biplane conversion—actually a sesquiplane, since the lower wing has less than half the area of the upper—was developed in 1966 for J-3s, PA-11s, and PA-18s by William G. Dorsch of Little Rock, Arkansas (Fig. 10-34). It was marketed as the Aeromod 100. It was intended originally as an agplane, but found other uses as a glider tug, bushplane, etc. Dorsch made four factory conversions and subsequently sells conversion kits to tandem-seat Cub owners.

Another cut-down fuselage modification similar to but not as extreme as that in Fig. 10-5, and with more practical application, is that of the J-5A Cub Coupe of Fig. 10-35, which is used for aerial photography.

Piper added carburetor and cabin heat controls to the engine exhaust system starting in 1939, but some private owners and small shops built their own as well as devising desirable cold-weather modifications for Cubs (Figs. 10-36 and 10-37).

10-34 A PA-18-135 converted to an Aeromod 100 by addition of a lower wing. Placard inside cockpit lists empty weight as 1187 pounds, gross weight as 2450 pounds.

10-35 This J-5A with wingtip plates has a cut-down rear fuselage to improve the field of view for air-to-air photography. The new flat window at the rear of the cabin opens to give the cameraman an unimpeded view.

10-36 A J-2 Cub with a post-delivery modification of the exhaust stacks to form heat muffs; probably one side for carburetor heat and the other for cabin heat.

10-37 Different J-2 exhaust modification with both sides feeding a single heat muff. Note sheet metal shielding to reduce air flow into engine and prevent overcooling in cold weather.

An outstanding example of several modifications applied simultaneously to the same airplane is the Alaska-based Super Cub shown in Fig. 10-38. It has a 180-hp engine, strut-braced horizontal tail, tundra tires, booster wingtips, military-type rear windows, doors on both sides of the fuselage, and clear-view panels installed in the bottoms of both doors, all intended to increase its utility.

10-38 This PA-18-180 probably incorporates more externally-visible modifications than can be found on any other Cub. See text for listing.

Most-extreme Cub modification

None of the Cub modifications shown so far have resulted in a shift of the original airplane center of gravity (C.G.). Even the biplane modifications have the added wing directly under the upper to keep the center of lift in the same longitudinal position relative to the original C.G.

The modification by Jack Yentzer of Sheridan, Wyoming (Fig. 10-39), built for high-altitude dusting and spraying, is the only one to result in a major shift of the C.G. Using a mix of J-3 and PA-18 parts, he replaced the 95-hp Continental C-90 engine (185 pounds bare) with a 200-hp Ranger 6-440-C2 engine and cowling from a war-surplus U.S. Army Fairchild PT-19 (376 pounds bare, plus cowling). To accommodate the resulting forward move of the C.G., the new lower wing was installed ahead of the upper wing to align the center

Leo J. Kohn

10-39 Jack Yentzer and his modified "Staggerwing Cub," N202A, reserialled 111 as the first General Airplane Services Model 11. Note Ranger engine under PT-19 cowling, forward location of lower wing to accommodate C.G. shift, revised strutting, and Whittaker landing gear.

of lift with the new C.G. position. The new configuration quickly earned the ship the nickname of "Staggerwing Cub," after the famous Beech Model 17 Staggerwing biplane.

Gross weight of the General Airplane Services Model 11, to use its official name, is 3000 pounds.

Truly, the Cub is the world's most-modified airplane.

11

Cubs in show business

The light weight, low power, and low-speed maneuverability of the Cub made it a natural for low level and close-in air show performances. Stock model and highly modified Cubs have predominated in this work for more than 50 years. Some of the specialized acts are described below.

Grandma and the Professor

One of the most popular and enduring acts is low-level "crazy flying." This starts in one of two ways. Someone is going to give an 80-year-old grandmother her first airplane ride. She is escorted, in sunbonnet and long dress, to the Cub and strapped into the back seat. The pilot then gets in and someone props it to start the engine. For some reason, however, the pilot gets out, leaving granny aboard with the engine running. You know what happens next! Granny hits the throttle and the plane runs away, seemingly out of control.

The plane runs all over the airport, hopping over obstacles, bouncing on one wheel and then the other, dragging a wingtip on the ground, etc. (Fig. 11-1). This goes on for 10 or 15 minutes, after which the plane taxies normally to the grandstands. "Granny" then steps out, soon to be identified as a well-known stunt pilot.

A minor variation is the "Professor," who maintains that flying has been done all wrong ever since the Wright Brothers, and that his method will change things. However, he needs an airplane in which to demonstrate his method. Finally, the powers-that-be agree to let him go up in a Cub—with a check pilot aboard. The rest of the act is pretty much as "Grandma," but with more actual air work. As practiced by the late Capt. Dick Schramm, USNR,

11-1 "The Crazy Professor," Navy Reserve Capt. Dick Schramm, drags a wingtip of a borrowed J-3C-65 Cub through the grass during one of his low-altitude air show performances.

the major part of the act was an almost unbelievable routine of low-level aerobatics in a most illogical airplane (Fig. 11-2).

One variation in Capt. Schramm's act was to have the Professor drop his "How to Fly" book out of the plane during takeoff. If the field was suitable, his son drove a car down the runway while a passenger handed the book up to the Professor, who was flying erratically alongside.

One of his favorite low-altitude maneuvers was what he called "The Whifferdill." This was a quarter-loop followed by a vertical half-roll and completion of the loop in the opposite direction.

A surprising thing about Capt. Schramm's show was that he did not have a special Cub of his own. He would borrow one from a local owner whenever he was to do a show in the area, startling the owner if he hadn't seen the act before.

World's smallest airport

Cubs and cars combined to make good acts. One of the earliest was to have an E-2 Cub take off from a platform on top of a car speeding down the runway at the Cub's flying speed. This act was billed as "The World's Smallest Airport" (Fig. 11-3) and was soon expanded to have the Cub land back on

11-2 This J-3C-65 at an air show does not have an inverted fuel system. "Professor" Schramm is performing a slow roll barely two wingspans off the ground.

the platform. With no wheel brakes on the early Cubs, this was tricky. Float-equipped Cubs did better; once down they didn't roll. Later, wheel brakes on J-3 Cubs and wells in the deck for the wheels made car-top landings easier (Fig. 11-4).

11-3 A J-2 Cub lifts off of a car billed as "The World's Smallest Airport" at a 1938 air show. The act soon expanded to include a landing back on the car.

11-4 A stock postwar J-3C-65 Cub used in the "World's Smallest Airport" act. Hydraulic brakes on the airplane and wheel wells, visible at the front of the platform, greatly simplify the landing-on process.

Car-to-plane pickups

One Cub-and-car stunt adopted from the early air circus days was the car-to-plane pickup. A man on the car would catch a rope ladder hanging from the Cub flying close overhead, and climb aboard (Fig. 11-5). The slow speed of the Cub made it much more suitable for this act than the old Jennies and Standards used in the early 1920s.

11-5 Another standard air show routine for the versatile Cub was this J-3C-65 picking up a passenger from the open car speeding down the runway.

As an extension of the car-to-plane pickup, the acrobat, who wore fire-proof clothing, helmet, and goggles, stayed on the ladder. After a circuit of the field, he would be pulled through a burning wooden framework that had been erected at the side of the runway (Fig. 11-6).

Dry landing seaplanes

A common act is to land a stock Cub floatplane on the grass in front of the crowd. This practice is fairly common with seaplane pilots, but for the public at

11-6 In a variation of the car-to-plane pickup act, the person picked up stays on the ladder and is then pulled through a blazing wooden framework. The plane is a PA-12 Cub Super Cruiser.

large it makes a good novelty act. Sometimes this plane is the one that had taken off from the car. In some cases, when the wind is right and the grass is wet, the Cub seaplane can take off again. Otherwise, it is hoisted on a dolly and hauled back to the water or, in some cases, put on a small wheeled carriage so it can use its own power to make a takeoff run on the unattached wheels, lifting off and leaving them on the ground (see page 109).

Other acts

Other Cub acts involve specially modified planes, some of which are so extensively altered that they are hardly recognizable as Cubs (see Chapter 8). These are used mainly for spectacular competition-type aerobatics. Others are modified for specific novelty airplane acts.

One, seen in the late 1930s, was the "Pic-A-Back Cubs" act. Two otherwise stock J-3Cs were lined up one on top of the other (Fig. 11-7). The landing gear of the lower unit was reinforced to support the extra weight. The two would take off as a single unit and go through a mild aerobatic routine. Following that, the two would break apart for further individual aerobatics and separate landings.

The most extreme air show modification of a Cub was made by Mike Murphy in the 1930s. He rebuilt a wrecked E-2 "upside down," with an open cockpit on the bottom and an additional landing gear and cockpit on top (Fig. 11-8). He took off and landed while suspended upside down in the lower cockpit.

Gordon S. Williams collection

11-7 The most unusual Cub air show act was the "Pic-a-Back Cubs" routine with two J-3Cs, one with a 75-hp engine and one with an 80-hp. Note the inverted fuselage lettering on the top Cub—it has an inverted fuel system and does an inverted flyby after separation.

Ken Sumney

11-8 In 1938 Mike Murphy rebuilt an E-2 Cub for an "upside down" air show act. He took off and landed inverted from the bottom cockpit. Even the tail registration number is painted on upside down.

Other acts feature Cubs stripped of their fuselage fabric for use in clown acts. Some perfectly stock models have small paper bags of flour taped under their wingtips. The pilot drags the wingtip on the ground to break the bag and release a big puff of white flour.

These are only a few uses of Cubs in show business. Other Cubs are fitted with inverted fuel systems for continuous inverted operation and a greater variety of acts (Fig. 11-9). Possibilities for other acts with Cubs are infinite.

11-9 A different inverted situation from that of Fig. 11-2. This photograph shows the top J-3C Cub of Fig. 11-7 with inverted fuel system performing another standard air show act—the inverted ribbon cut. It requires a long straight approach in inverted flight.

12

Cubs at work and play

Although the Cub originated as a trainer and sportplane, and was long produced as such, its versatility eventually put it to work in other fields. Although the attrition rate in some of the specialized lines of work is quite high, the durability of the Cub airframe ensures that Cubs will be used for work and for play many years after the last Cub is built.

Working Cubs

Well into the 1950s old J-3s were the mainstay of the light-weight end of the crop dusting and spraying business. Soon after the Super Cub appeared, many were built specifically for that work (Figs. 12-1 and 12-2).

Other Super Cubs, fitted with extra equipment at the factory or by the customer, are used by such specialized organizations as the U.S. Border Patrol (Fig. 12-3) and the Alaska State Troopers (Figs. 12-4 and 12-5). Others go to private firms for pipeline and powerline patrol, fish spotting (Fig. 12-6), and many routine business uses. Some fixed-base operators (FBOs) started using three-place J-5 Cub Cruisers as air taxis before WWII and continued with PA-12s and PA-14s afterward (Fig. 12-7).

Cubs are widely used also for two kinds of towing. They make excellent glider tugs (Fig. 12-8), especially when fitted with larger than standard engines, and earn good money for their owners in the boring job of towing banners. Equipment for towing is simple—a quick-release towhook on the tail wheel bracket operated by a cord or cable running to the cabin on the outside of the fuselage. For all towing operations, a waiver is required from the FAA. A related business that uses some Cubs is skywriting (Fig. 12-9).

12-1 A PA-18A-125 Super Cub duster at working altitude, its wheels just above the row crops.

12-2 Sprayers work at slightly higher altitudes than dusters. This sprayer is another PA-18A-125.

12-3 Super Cubs have long been a mainstay of the U.S. Border Patrol along the Mexican border. This PA-18-150 with special markings is over Mexican territory at Juarez, just across the Rio Grande River from El Paso, Texas.

Ever since the days of the E-2, the open right side of the tandem-seat Cub cabin has made it a natural for aerial photography, either of the ground or of other airplanes flying alongside. Many of the flight views in this book were shot from Cubs.

Even unmodified Cubs can do heroic work. Super Cubs can carry just about everything that can be packed into them while others, even 65-hp J-3s, can carry surprisingly large external cargo (Fig. 12-10).

In less spectacular but equally important ways, the stock 65-hp J-3s carried on their primary work as trainers well into the postwar years. The best-known program, of course, was the CPTP operation of 1939–1944. This gave college students eight hours of primary training, but oddly, did not let them solo.

Recreational Cubs

Cubs are used in a wide variety of recreational areas, some of which are difficult to separate from professional use. An example is the Cub used to hunt

12-4 Cockpit of an Alaska State Trooper PA-18-150 shows some of the extra instrumentation and electronic gear installed in the Super Cub for that organization's specialized work.

12-5 An Alaska Trooper checks a fisherman's papers in the course of a routine patrol in his PA-18-150S.

12-6 Most working Cubs operate from fixed bases. This fishing boat becomes a mobile base and the PA-18-150 seaplane goes with it to spot schools of fish after being launched overside for a water takeoff.

12-7 A PA-12 Super Cruiser used as an aerial taxi. Note the name "Piper Taxicub" on the fuselage.

12-8 Super Cubs are the most widely used towplanes in the American soaring movement. This PA-18-125 tows a Schweizer 1-26 sailplane at Tehachapi, California.

coyotes and other predators from the air for sport or bounty and the Cub used by game workers or others to control predators. Recreational pilots use Cubs for transportation to hunting or fishing areas, and fishermen sometimes cast a line right from their airplanes (Fig. 12-11). I found that a Cub drifting downwind in a mild breeze moves at about the right speed for trolling. Sometimes the recreational use of a Cub is a very spur-of-the-moment operation to take advantage of a unique situation (Fig. 12-12).

12-9 This modified PA-12 with a 150-hp Lycoming engine, named "Smokey," was used as a skywriter for more than 25 years by Seattle owner Art Bell. Note the smoke generator tube.

Steve McCutcheon via Alaska Aviation Heritage Museum

12-10 Cargo that can't fit into a Cub can be carried outside. This 1945 J-3C-65S carries a canoe that is longer than the floats.

Piper

12-11 Some sportsmen fish from their airplanes. Small planes like this J-3F-65 can be better than a boat for trying widely separated spots on a large lake.

Max Witters

12-12 A rare snowstorm closed the airport at Renton, Washington, to wheeled planes, so Witters Flying Service put a J-3C-65 on skis and had the field to itself for a day of fun.

Endurance flights

One very specialized use of Cubs, which is hard to define as either professional or recreational, is the endurance flight. Up to the mid-1930s, most endurance attempts involved aerial refueling from a hose lowered by a tanker
airplane. When Cubs and other lightplanes got into the act, a new method of
refueling was introduced.

This new refueling method involved flying the plane above an automobile
speeding down an airport runway. One of the two people in the airplane would
lower a line and a helper in the car would hook on a five-gallon can of gasoline
or whatever supplies were needed, which was then hauled up and into the airplane (Fig. 12-13). In some cases, the transfer of supplies was simplified by the
use of seaplanes—the supplies could be placed in a rack on the right-hand float.
This called for more precise flying than when using the lowered-line method.

Russell Phelinger collection

12-13 Lightplane endurance flights of the late 1930s were refueled by pickups from
automobiles. This J-3C-50 "Little Bear" set an American and world record for lightplanes
at 218 hours 23 minutes, October 23–November 2, 1938.

Auto-refueled endurance flights with J-2 Cubs began in July 1937, with a 24 hour 20 minute flight, and were mostly for men's or women's records in the lightplane category. Such flights could be regarded as competitive sport. Others, with sponsors whose names appear on the sides and wings of the airplane, could be considered as professional operations.

The first really notable use of a Cub for such a refueled flight was a publicity flight from Newark, New Jersey to Miami, Florida and return non-stop, May 17–19, 1938. The flight was not for an endurance record but to cover the distance. The plane was a J-3P, NX20280, with pickup refuelings at two points enroute and at Miami. The flight took 63 hours 54 minutes, covered 2310 statute miles, and used 223 gallons of gas.

There is a J-3P with a similar number flying today, but it is not the same plane. Today's plane is a converted J-3C-65 fitted with the rare Lenape Papoose engine and the 1938 J-3P's registration number.

In one case, a J-3 was specially modified to permit minor engine maintenance in flight. "Miss Dairylea," a J-3F-50, NX20261, stayed up for 106 hours 6 minutes, September 2–6, 1938, to set a men's world lightplane record. The windshield could be opened to permit a crewman to reach the engine and change spark plugs (Fig. 12-14).

12-14 Some Cubs, like this J-3F-50 "Miss Dairylea," here setting a men's landplane endurance record of 106 hours, 6 minutes September 2–6, 1938, were modified to permit minor inflight maintenance. Note also the belly fuel tank and the radio antenna.

The longest Cub endurance flight took a full month to accomplish and set a world's record for all aircraft classes at 726 hours. The plane was a J-3C-50 seaplane, NX23233, and the dates were September 30–October 30, 1939 (Fig. 12-15). The flight used 3000 gallons of gas and 75 gallons of oil, hoisted during 1547 pickups. Distance covered was 55,000 statute miles.

12-15 This J-3C-50S set the world's endurance record for all classes of aircraft at 726 hours between September 30 and October 30, 1939.

13

Cub look-alikes

The world-wide popularity of the Cub quickly reinforced the old saying: "Imitation is the sincerest form of flattery." The Cub inspired many imitators almost as soon as the J-2 appeared (Fig. 13-1). Since one of the first was in Japan, it did nothing to debunk the then prevailing myth that the Japanese could only copy foreign designs in the years before WWII.

Other nations also developed Cub look-alikes in general proportions but not enough exact detail to be called outright copies. The Brazilian Paulista CAP-4 Paulistinha (Fig. 13-2) is a representative example of several Cub clones developed by the world aviation industry.

A somewhat different situation prevailed in the U.S. after the Super Cub went out of production. Unable to buy the design of the Super Cub from

13-1 The Japanese Nozawa Z-1 was the first of numerous Cub look-alikes. The only notable outward differences are in the landing gear and the vertical tail shape.

13-2 The Brazilian Paulista CAP-4 Paulistinha greatly resembles the Piper PA-11, even to the color arrangement. This example, one of 782 built between 1942 and 1949, was imported into the U.S. and given an experimental license.

Piper to fill a perceived market demand, Christen Industries of Afton, Wyoming, developed its own A-1 "Husky" model closely along Super Cub lines. The engine is a 180-hp Lycoming O-360-C1G. The first flight was in 1986 (Fig. 13-3). The Husky is in regular production as a certificated commercial airplane.

The sport aviation activity has also produced a number of Cub look-alikes (Figs. 13-4 and 13-5). Many are scaled-down and somewhat out-of-proportion ultralights but one, the Wag-Aero "CubY," is as close a duplicate of the J-3 Cub as can be made (Fig. 13-6).

The CubY began as a kit-plane project for the amateur airplane builder in order to use up an enormous supply of surplus military L-4 parts that an airline pilot, Richard H. Wagner, had bought. The resulting airplane first flew in 1974, and to date more than 2300 kits have been sold world-wide.

The kit-built CubY differs from the J-3 in a few small details for the benefit of the home builder. The wing ribs are built of wood and longitudinal trim is by means of a tab in the left elevator instead of by a jackscrew and movable stabilizer. The tab and the absence of the fuselage slot at the leading edge of the stabilizer are about the only external details that distinguish the CubY from the J-3.

13-3 The Christen Husky was designed to carry on the work of the Super Cub after Piper discontinued that model. While the resemblance is strong, the 180-hp Husky is not an exact Cub copy.

13-4 A Canadian homebuilt that appears to have been assembled from cut-down J-3 Cub parts. Note the entirely different exhaust system on the Lycoming engine.

13-5 "Yellow III" is the name builder Bud McHolland gave to his PA-11 look-alike. Major change is to a new wing planform with a more modern NACA 23012 airfoil and a Continental O-200 engine with three-blade propeller. This one is Bud's third PA-11 look-alike.

13-6 Most accurate Cub look-alike, and freely acknowledged as such, is the Wag-Aero "CubY," which started out to use many surplus J-3/L-4 parts. This 1974 prototype is painted Cub Yellow on the right side and green and yellow on the left.

Wagner sells the kits through his company, Wag-Aero, P.O. Box 181, Lyon, Wisconsin. He also has developed a kit-plane clone of the four-place Piper PA-14 Family Cruiser. Although duplicating certificated airplanes in most details, planes built from Wag-Aero kits are homebuilts and licensed in the amateur-built subcategory of the experimental category, with attendant restrictions on their usage.

14

The antique airplane boom

Until the early 1950s anyone who flew an old airplane, generally meaning pre-WWII lightplanes or certain war-surplus trainers, did so because he couldn't afford anything better. Owners of such junk cheapies were often low-budget pilots and pilots with new commercial licenses eager to build up their flight hours quickly so they could get airline or other jobs that called for a certain number of hours.

Such planes were flown intensively until their annual licenses expired. For many, the cost of the work required to get the planes past the inspector could easily be more than its market value. In such cases, they simply abandoned the airplane or at least stripped it for parts.

Organized antiques

In the early 1950s, the picture changed. Old airplanes suddenly acquired status as representatives of a bygone era, and the antique airplane boom began. Soon there was a national organization—The Antique Airplane Association, or AAA (Antique Airfield, Route 2, Box 172, Ottumwa, Iowa, 52501)—which kept members in touch through its magazine.

Now that old had become fashionable, the AAA held national fly-ins specifically for antiques. It also established standards for classification and was able to influence the FAA to the point that the agency recognizes antique airplanes for what they are and allows special exemptions from standard civil airplane marking regulations so that a restored 1940 airplane can carry accurate markings for that time.

More importantly, the AAA helps owners of many antique production and orphaned models to find needed replacement parts through its head-quarters. As the organization grew, it formed unofficial "type clubs," networks of owners of a particular make or model of airplane. These are aeronautical mutual aid societies that sometimes hold fly-ins of their own.

Functions similar to those of the AAA are performed by the Experimental Aircraft Association (EAA), which was formed about the same time as the AAA, but was concerned initially with homebuilt airplanes. In later years, EAA expanded its coverage and now has an "antique and classic" division (EAA Antique/Classic Division, EAA Aviation Center, P. O. Box 3086, Oshkosh, WI 54903-3086). This division parallels the AAA activity, with its own type clubs and the division's own national magazine. Military Cub models like the L-4 and the HE/AE-1 also qualify for EAA's Warbird Division (Fig. 14-1).

14-1 Popularity of the Warbird portion of the antique airplane movement resulted in many Cubs being given WWII markings and colors. This PA-12 carries accurate 1943 camouflage while representing a Navy AE-1 ambulance plane.

Both organizations are in general agreement on the definition of an antique airplane. The FAA and AAA go along with an airplane over 30 years old being an antique. EAA is more selective. It defines an antique as any plane built before the end of WWII. Those built from 1946 through 1954 are defined as "classics" and are judged separately within the antique classic division.

Two separate national organizations for Cubs are the Cub Club (c/o John Bergson, P. O. Box 2002, Mt. Pleasant, MI 48858), which emphasizes the antique aspect of the Cub, and the Super Cub Pilot's Association (c/o Jim Richmond, P. O. Box 9823, Yakima, WA 98909), concerned mainly with increasing the utility of the Super Cub through upgrades, bigger engines, etc.

The antique J-3

When the antique boom began, J-3 Cubs, only recently out of production, were not as big a part of it as their actual numbers would imply. Many of them were still working as trainers in flying schools. Although not fitting the yet-to-be-adopted 30-year criterion, the E-2s, J-2s, J-4s and J-5s were regarded as antiques when the movement began (Fig. 14-2).

14-2 Taylor E-2s are the rarest items in the antique Cub fleet. Of 351 E-2/F-2s built, only 27 survive today.

As the movement grew the J-3s, and surplus L-4s that were licensed as J-3s, became increasingly active in the two organizations to the point where they are now the most numerous single model in either one. While Super Cubs built before 1962 qualify as genuine antiques, they are not nearly as well represented in the over-all antique movement as are the J-3s (Fig. 14-3).

Because almost all J-3s left the factory painted Cub Yellow (although commonly called that, the proper name is Lock Haven Yellow), about the first thing an owner of a well-used example did when it needed recovering or repainting was to pick any color other than yellow. Now that J-3s have reached a minimum age of 45 years and practically cult status, great effort is made to restore them to factory-new appearance—Cub Yellow, lightning stripe, Cub decal on the fin, and old-style NC registration numbers on the wings and rudder.

For a while, surplus L-4s that retained their extra glasswork were painted as ordinary airplanes. More recently, more and more of them are becoming part of the warbird movement and are being restored to original military color and markings. Unfortunately, there is much room for error with these. Idealistic, rather than authentic, colors and markings seem to be the rule (Fig. 14-4).

14-3 A beautifully restored J-3C-65 Cub participating in an antique airplane fly-in on a private grass airstrip.

14-4 A war-surplus L-4H with restored wartime color and markings seen at a French antique airplane fly-in. As with many such restorations, the insignia proportions are off, and although the army serial number on the tail is correct for the airplane, it should not have the initial 4 and the style of the figures is incorrect.

Some modern improvements are adopted, such as MacCauley metal propellers, sensitive altimeters, and in many cases (of necessity) small or even hand-held battery radios.

Latter-day equipment loses points for contestants in antique judging, so some owners remove their metal propellers and put on old wooden ones, and remove other modern items when going to an antique fly-in. In the opposite direction, Cub owners in search of maximum authenticity work hard to acquire the original instruments that were produced with the Cub logo. Previous owners may have replaced these with more up-to-date instruments for utility, not antique, use of their Cubs.

One latter-day Cub owner went backward in time so far as to modify his L-4H to look like a J-2 (Fig. 14-5). Some J-2 owners in other countries have been able to obtain those countries' approval for installing 65-hp Continental A-65 engines in their upgraded Cubs (Fig. 14-6).

14-5 Some owners try to convert their Cubs to other models. This surplus L-4H in France has been modified to resemble a J-2 by changing the vertical tail surfaces and the cabin windows.

The FAA ruling in the 1960s that airplanes over 30 years old could use the old-style registration number applications caught some J-3 owners unhappily in the middle. Pre–WWII Cubs could use the old application; those built afterward were not yet old enough and were stuck with the 12-inch fuselage figures decreed in 1966.

14-6 A British-registered Taylor J-2, C/N 997, upgraded for present-day flying by installation of a 65-hp Continental A65 engine, a modification not permitted under U.S. regulations.

Since then, the ruling that anything that looks like an old airplane can use the old application still leaves some J-3 owners unhappy. They can get rid of the big fuselage numbers, but painting them out results in a mismatch of new and old coloring that is more unsightly than the big numbers. The cost of repainting the whole airplane just to revert to the old style is not worth it except for the most dedicated purists.

At this writing, the J-3 Fleet, including L-4s, consists of slightly over 4200 Cubs.

Special Cub activity

There is one national-scale activity organized for antique Taylor/Piper airplanes, but is attended mostly by J-3s because of their overwhelming numbers. This is the "Sentimental Journey" to Lock Haven, Pennsylvania, birthplace of most of the Cubs. This started in 1986 as a nonprofit operation that annually draws participants from most states, including Alaska. It is a week-long summer gathering of antique Taylor and Piper airplanes, well-supported by the community, featuring meetings, seminars, tours of the Piper Aviation Museum, and local sightseeing trips. Although intended primarily for Taylors and Pipers, other makes are welcome.

For information concerning future Sentimental Journeys, contact Sentimental Journey Inc., P. O. Box J-3 (how appropriate!), Lock Haven, PA 17745-0496; (717) 398-1102.

The replacement parts problem

As with all out-of-production vehicles, owners are faced with the problem of finding needed replacement parts. The AAA/EAA Type Clubs are a big help in finding original parts from old scrapped or abandoned airplanes. Cub owners are fortunate in having available two sources of new parts.

UNIVAIR Aircraft Corporation (2500 Himalaya Road, Aurora, CO 80011) has both the type certificates of a number of different discontinued airplanes as well as the certificates for accessories like propellers. For J-3 Cubs, UNIVAIR began building some parts under FAA Parts Manufacturing Approvals, or PMAs. These allow the making of parts by a builder who does not have the type certificate for that particular airplane. About half of UNIVAIR's PMA business is for ragwing Piper models from the J-3 through the PA-25 Pawnee agplane.

Another source of PMA Cub parts is Wag-Aero (see Chapter 13). Wag-Aero can provide a complete welded steel tube fuselage assembly for a certificated J-3, plus many lesser assemblies.

Idol with feet of clay

For all its charisma and fame as everyone's ideal airplane for fun flying to workhorse, the Cub is far from perfect in its structure and installations. This is not a situation exclusive to Cubs; it is a trait shared by practically every other production model airplane in the world.

From time to time various weaknesses or design deficiencies such as installations that result in parts chafing, sub-standard materials, or quality-control errors become known to the manufacturer. The immediate result is the issuance of a Service Bulletin that discusses the problem, the serial numbers of the airplanes affected, and the recommended fix. For an in-production model the shortcoming is corrected in-house on subsequent C/Ns.

In some cases the shortcoming might not show up for several years of hard wear but still can be the subject of a Service Bulletin, either fleet-wide or directed to specific C/Ns. In other cases, the trouble becomes the concern of the government, which then issues Airworthiness Directives, or AD Notes, that have the authority of law to force compliance. Some of these require compliance within a certain number of flight hours after issuance, others by a specified calendar date. Really serious situations can call for immediate grounding of the airplane until the fix is accomplished.

Representative examples of some of the simplest AD notes are presented here:

46-37-02 PIPER: (Was mandatory Note 13 of AD-691-2.) Applies to J3C-65, J3C-65S, Serial Numbers 14027 Through 17959, Inclusive.

Compliance required immediately.

Affected airplanes should be examined immediately to ascertain that the fuel strainer is properly installed. The strainer should be installed with the IN port adjacent to the firewall and the OUT port facing the carburetor. If the strainer is not installed as above, it should be reversed for proper fuel flow.

(Piper Service Bulletin No. 91 covers this same subject.)

48-03-03 PIPER: Applies to PA-11 Aircraft Serial Numbers 11-1 Through 11-301, and 11-1350 Through 11-1400, Except Serial Numbers 11-233, 11-243, 11-261, 11-266, 11-281, 11-296, and 11-300.

Compliance required by April 1, 1948.

In order to prevent engine malfunctioning due to insufficient fuel flow when less than 5 gallons of fuel are in the wing tank and the airplane is operated in prolonged glides and dives, a header tank (Piper P/N 10725) must be installed in the fuel system. Until the header tank is installed, avoid prolonged glides and dives when less than 5 gallons fuel are in the main tank. (Piper Service Bulletin No. 99 dated July 29, 1947, covers this subject.)

54-19-01 PIPER: Applies to Models PA-18 and PA-18A Restricted Category Aircraft With Dusting Venturi, Up to and including Serial Number 18-3752.

Compliance required not later than October 15, 1954.

There have been several instances of excessive CO concentration in the cockpit when the dusting venturi is used. Such contamination has serious adverse effects upon pilot reaction. To prevent CO from entering the cockpit, a new trim plate should be installed and a new brake line cover plate should be placed over the brake line where the line enters the bottom of the fuselage.

(Piper Service Letter No. 225, dated August 23, 1954, covers the same subject.)

53-04-01 PIPER: Applies to All Model PA-18 Aircraft Which Have Not Had the Control Stick Retention Device Modified to Incorporate a Through Bolt.

Compliance required by April 1, 1953.

In order to prevent the control stick inadvertently pulling out of the socket, continue the existing hole for the retention pin on the quick detachable control stick spring device through the control stick and socket and install an AN 3-14 or AN 3-14A through bolt.

(Piper Service Letter No. 162 dated March 6, 1951, covers this same subject.)

15

Death and rebirth of the Piper Cub

Piper continued to mark milestones. It delivered its 100,000th airplane, a twin-engine PA-31 Cheyenne, in April 1976, but celebrated the occasion by painting a Super Cub with old J-3 color and markings and decorating its nose with the words "100,000 Cubs" (Fig. 15-1).

Piper also got caught up in the rash of big-business takeovers of American airplane manufacturers. In 1977, Chris-Craft, a major manufacturer of powerboats, and Bangor Punta Corporation, began a fight for control of Piper by buying up outstanding shares of Piper stock at above-market prices. Bangor Punta won, and made Piper a subsidiary in 1979.

Business began to decline in 1980.

In 1981 WTA Incorporated of Lubbock, Texas, distributor of Piper Super Cubs and the PA-25 Pawnee and PA-36 Brave agplanes, worked out an arrangement with Piper to become the world-wide distributor for the Super Cub and the Brave. WTA then bought Piper's entire inventory of both models. When the Super Cubs were all sold, WTA got Piper to build an additional 50, the last of which was completed early in 1983. No more Super Cubs were built at Lock Haven. The tooling was stored and it looked like the last of some 9401 civil and military Super Cubs had been built.

WTA then sought to buy the tooling and the Type Certificate for the Super Cub. Piper was receptive to the idea, but insisted on WTA carrying $100,000,000 worth of product liability insurance covering all Super Cubs built since 1950. No deal was made, and the absence of the Super Cub from the market resulted in the creation of the Christen Husky (see Chapter 13).

In the 1980s Piper, along with other manufacturers of general aviation airplanes, suffered from a major downturn in sales. This was complicated by the

15-1 Piper completed the 100,000th Piper airplane in 1976. Although it was a twin-engine Cheyenne model, the company publicized the event by painting a PA-18-150 Super Cub like the classic J-3 with the legend "100,000 Pipers" on the nose.

growing flood of product liability suits brought against the manufacturers. These suits cited faulty design as the cause of a wide range of usually fatal accidents. Under prevailing American law, a manufacturer who successfully defends such a suit, often inaugurated by the plaintiff on a lawyer-contingency basis, cannot recover court costs from the plaintiff. This forces the manufacturers to carry product liability insurance at such high rates that it adds several thousand dollars to the cost of each airplane, a serious deterrent to sales.

With the decline of general aviation business, Bangor Punta sold Piper to Lear Siegler in 1984. Under the new ownership, operations were moved to the modern Piper plant in Vero Beach, Florida and the Lock Haven plant was closed. Super Cub tooling remained in storage there. The Super Cub had already been discontinued in 1981 but managed to hang on for a year under unusual circumstances.

The change of ownership did not bring prosperity to Piper. On May 12, 1987, the firm was bought by M. Stuart Millar, a California businessman, who became sole owner. His intention was to resume production of several discontinued Piper models, including the Super Cub (Fig. 15-2), and had the tooling brought from Lock Haven to Vero Beach. Two Super Cubs were built in 1988, starting with C/N 1809001; but only six in 1990 and none in 1991.

Millar proposed a new and unique sales opportunity for the Super Cub. In addition to the normal factory-built airplane, he would offer a kit with many factory-built components that the customer could complete himself. This would not be a "homebuilt" airplane flown on an experimental license, but a fully-licensed standard-category airplane. The proposed kit price, less engine

15-2 When the Super Cub was put back in production in 1988 after a five-year hiatus, it appeared in the all-yellow color scheme and unique markings of the famous J-3, even to application of the old Cub logo to the tail.

and propeller, was $21,095 when the 1988 factory-built Super Cub was selling for $42,595.

The kit never came to market. After one, C/N 1809033, was built by Piper employees the kit program was dropped.

Business continued to decline in spite of Millar's changes, and Piper was forced into bankruptcy in July 1991. Under Chapter 11 of the U.S. bankruptcy laws, a company is allowed to remain in business while being protected from creditors' claims that if allowed would shut it down. The bankruptcy court allowed limited production of several Piper models for 1992, including three Super Cubs.

This Cub was delivered May 22, 1992, and at that time was expected to be the last American-built Cub. Since then, however, authorization has been obtained for additional Super Cubs to be built at Vero Beach.

The possibility of Cub production continuing outside of the United States has existed for several years. In 1990 negotiations were underway for the French manufacturer Aerospatiale to buy Piper and transfer its product line to France. This fell through, but at this writing, June 1992, two separate organizations in Canada, one in the Province of Saskatchewan and one in British Columbia, are negotiating the purchase of Piper and its transfer to Canada.

As this book reached production in early 1993, Piper revealed that it delivered two 1992 Super Cubs in January—serial numbers 1809059 and 1809061. A spokesman for the company said Piper will build 17 Super Cubs in 1993 and is expecting to emerge from Chapter 11 bankruptcy early in 1993.

16

J-3 Cub
color and markings

A few J-3s were delivered with special paint schemes, but the majority were all yellow in the shade that became universally known as Cub Yellow but was actually called Lock Haven Yellow.

The yellow J-3s do not all look alike in black-and-white photographs. The two matched photos of Figs. 16-1 and 16-2 illustrate this. Both were taken of the same airplane at almost the same time on the same photo flight at the same camera angle and under the same lighting conditions. Photo 16-1 was taken with panchromatic film and a yellow filter, as were most Piper publicity and record photos. This combination makes yellow appear quite light on photo prints. Photo 16-2 was taken on orthochromatic film and without a filter, making the yellow look quite dark.

Fuselage stripes

The early J-3s had a single black stripe running the full length of the fuselage on either side. This stripe tapered from a width of about two inches at the nose straight to a point on the rudder. A small barb was on the lower side of the front end of the stripe. Soon after the J-3Cs, Fs, Ls, and Ps appeared, the front end of the fuselage stripe was changed to a zig-zag lightning streak that ended at the rudder post.

Over the years the proportions of the zig-zag have varied, as has the actual location of the forward end of the marking relative to the fuselage. This is evident in photos throughout this book.

The absence of accurate information on the details of the zig-zag leave the owners/restorers of J-3s on their own as to just how to lay-out this distinctive

16-1 A J-3F-65 photographed on panchromatic film with a yellow filter. Note how light the Cub Yellow appears in black-and-white prints.

16-2 The same J-3F-65 photographed at the same time and under the same lighting conditions, but with orthochromatic film and no filter. Note how dark the yellow shows up in the print.

marking. Figure 16-3 shows a few individual variations photographed at the 1983 EAA fly-in at Oshkosh, Wisconsin, by National Air & Space Museum Curator Robert Mikesh.

Figure 16-4 is adapted from a J-3 Cub marking drawing provided

16-3 Variations of the Cub lightning streak seen on restored J-3s at the 1983 EAA convention. The bottom right is the most accurate.

by UNIVAIR and can be considered to be the official detail and position guide for the fuselage marking. Note that the reference lines for the zig-zag in Fig. 16-4 are relative to the lower window sill (parallel to the airplane center line), not the top of the stripe, which slopes slightly upward toward the tail.

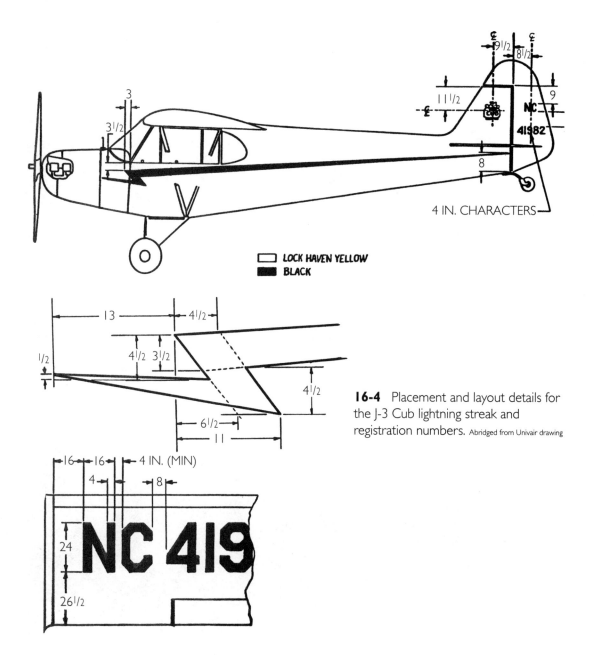

LOCK HAVEN YELLOW
BLACK

16-4 Placement and layout details for the J-3 Cub lightning streak and registration numbers. Abridged from Univair drawing

Registration numbers

Registration numbers in the production days of the J-3 and the PA-11 had the NC prefix instead of the N-only that dates from late 1948. On the Cubs, these were/are standard black block figures 24 inches high and 16 inches wide (width is ⅔ height). The width of the strokes is four inches, or ⅙ the height. Spacing between figures is also four inches. Piper made a notable exception in one place—the space between the letter C on the wing and the first number. This was just twice the normal spacing, as shown in the drawing of Fig. 16-4 and the photo of Fig. 16-5. Location was on the upper right and lower left wing and on each side of the rudder until the mandate for 12-inch numbers on the fuselage in 1966. The old style is now legal for all Cubs, even Super Cubs, since they are so similar to the older models.

16-5 The same J-3F-65 of Figs. 16-1 and 16-2 banked over to show the extra spacing between the NC and the numbers that was peculiar to Piper. It also applied to PA-11 Cub Specials.

Figure 16-4 shows also the correct location for the Cub logo on the fin and the four-inch block figures on the rudder.

Military markings

The U.S. military insignia varied in detail during WWII and afterward, and also moved slightly from the standard locations, so photographs of the particular military Cub being restored are the best guide. Proportions of the insignia were/are very exact, however, and are often laid out incorrectly by restorers. The correct proportions, and correct details for various time periods, are shown in Fig. 16-6.

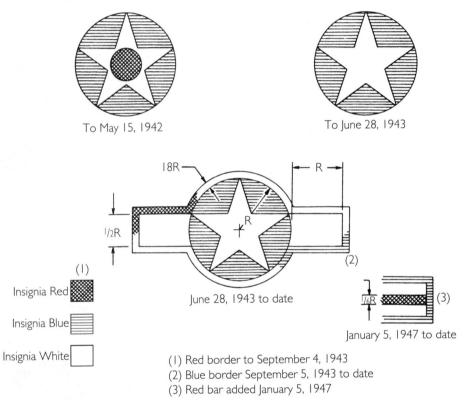

To May 15, 1942

To June 28, 1943

(1)

Insignia Red

Insignia Blue

Insignia White

18R

R

1/2R

(2)

R

June 28, 1943 to date

1/6R

(3)

January 5, 1947 to date

(1) Red border to September 4, 1943
(2) Blue border September 5, 1943 to date
(3) Red bar added January 5, 1947

16-6 Changes in the U.S. star-in-circle marking during the U.S. military career of the Piper Cub.

U.S. Army Cub markings

At the time the first YO-59s were delivered, camouflaged army airplanes had the national star on the upper left and lower right wing wingtips (just the opposite of civil registration numbers) and on both sides of the rear fuselage. Uncamouflaged army planes had the stars on both wings and no fuselage stars, but this did not apply to the O-59s and J-4s, all of which were camouflaged. Standard army camouflage was dark olive drab on top and side surfaces and medium gray on under surfaces. See Chapter 5 for further detail. By the time late L-4Hs and Js were being delivered in silver finish, the star on one wing and either side of the fuselage was standard.

U.S. Navy Cub markings

The NE-1s and HE-1s were delivered to the navy in over-all chrome yellow (similar to Cub yellow), which was the standard for navy primary trainers and ambulance planes at the time. Some that served overseas or in U.S. defense zones were given standard navy camouflage (Fig. 16-7). The uncamouflaged ones had stars on both wingtips and no fuselage stars until the arrangement of stars on upper left and lower right wing and each side of the fuselage was made standard for all U.S. military airplanes in February 1943.

16-7 The navy NE-1s were normally all yellow, but some used in U.S. defense zones received standard navy blue-gray camouflage on top and some side surfaces and light gray elsewhere. Stars were added to sides of fuselage for camouflaged airplanes in 1941, before that location became standard for all in February, 1943.

Trainers and other noncombat types were slow to pick up on such changes, and some NE-1s got to the end of WWII without acquiring fuselage stars. The NE-2s were transfers from army L-4J contracts and carried army camouflage and appropriate insignia distribution.

Cubs with invasion stripes

The unique "invasion stripes" used by the Allies for the July 1944 invasion of Europe and subsequent campaigns through the crossing of the Rhine in 1945 are quite popular for L-4s restored to wartime markings.

For all aircraft involved, these consisted of three white and two black stripes completely encircling the fuselage as shown in Fig. 16-8, and were applied chordwise on both surfaces of the wing starting at the inner end of the aileron and going outboard. On L-4s, the stripes were all nine inches wide.

Richard E. Smith

16-8 An L-4H "Maytag Messerschmitt" with invasion stripes photographed in a French meadow shortly after D-Day, June 6, 1944. The venturi tube under the nose operated gyro instruments that were not standard equipment for L-4s.

It should be noted that these stripes were applied hurriedly by hand to thousands of airplanes in a period of one day, and were not carefully masked and sprayed as is usually done for warbird restorations and museum displays. After the Normandy invasion, the stripes were removed from the upper wing surface and the top half of the fuselage.

Specifications
and performance
Taylor and Piper Cubs
through PA-18

These tables have been abridged, with minor corrections and additions, from those appearing in TAB book #2457, *The Piper Classics*, by the late Joe Christy. Two tables not included in that volume, covering the Taylor J-2 and the unlettered Piper J-3, have been added for this more-specialized volume.

Table A-1. Specifications and performance—Taylor E-2, J-2, and Piper J-3

	E-2	J-2	J-3	J-3C-50	J-3C-65	J-3P-50
Engine	Cont A-40-2	Cont A-40-4	Cont A-40-4**	Cont A-50	Cont A-65-8	Lenape LM-3
Hp and rpm	37 @ 2550	37 @ 2550	40 @ 2575	50 @ 1900	65 @ 2350	50 @ 2125
Gross weight (lbs.)	925	970	1000	1100	1220	1100
Empty weight (lbs.)	532	563	574	635	680	630
Useful load (lbs.)	393	407	426	465	540	470
Wingspan (ft.)	35.25	35.25	35.25	35.25	35.25	35.25
Wing area (sq. ft.)	184	178	178	178	178.5	178
Length (ft.)	22.25	22.4	22.4	22.25	22.4	22.3
Height (in.)	78	80	80	80	80	80
Chord (in.)	63	63	63	63	72	63
Power loading (lbs./hp)	25	26.2	25	22	18.75	22
Wing loading (lbs./sq. ft.)	5.03	5.44	5.6	6.18	6.84	6.18
Baggage capacity (lbs.)	5*	20	20	20	20	20
Fuel capacity (U.S. gal.)	9	9	9	12	12	12
Maximum speed (mph)	70	85	84	90	87	92
Cruise (mph)	62	70	70	80	73	80
Stalling speed (mph)	28	29	30	35	38	35
Rate of climb (initial; ft./min.)	400	450	400	500	450	500
Service ceiling (ft.)	12,000	12,000	—	10,000	11,500	12,000
Cruising range (statute mi.)	180	200	216	250	220	270
Fuel consumption (gal./hr.)	2.7	3.0	3.0	3.5	4.08	3.5

* Only if approved baggage compartment installed.

** Also Franklin 4AC-150 Series 40, 40 hp @ 1875 rpm

Table A-2. Specifications and performance—Piper J-4 and J-5 series

Engines	J-4 Cont A-50-1	J-4A Cont A-65	J-4E Cont A-75	J-4F Lyc O-145	J-5A/J-5B Cont A-75-8 Lyc GO-145	J-5C-100 Lyc O-235-2
Hp and rpm	50 @ 1900	65 @ 2350	75 @ 2600	55 @ 2300	75 @ 2600 75 @ 3200	100 @ 2550
Gross weight (lbs.)	1200	1300	1400	1200	1450	1550
Empty weight (lbs.)	710	740	865	720	820	860
Useful load (lbs.)	490	560	535	480	630	890
Wingspan (ft.)	36.12	36.12	36.12	36.12	35.5	35.5
Wing area (sq. ft.)	183	183	183	183	179.3	179.3
Length (ft.)	22.5	22.5	22.5	22.5	22.5	22.5
Height (in.)	82	82	82	82	82	82
Propeller diameter (max. in.)	63	63	63	63	74	74
Power loading (lbs./hp)	24	20	18.66	21.8	19.3	15.5
Wing Loading (lbs./sq. ft.)	6.55	7.1	6.55	6.55	8.09	8.64
Baggage capacity (lbs.)	105	116	116	105	41	41
Fuel capacity (U.S. gal.)	16	25	25	16	25	20
Tire size	8.00x4	8.00x4	8.00x4	8.00x4	8.00x4	8.00x4
Maximum speed (mph)	93	100	105	95	95	110
Cruising (mph @ 3,000 ft.)	83	92	96	85	80	95
Stalling speed (mph)	35	37	40	35	43	45
Rate of climb (initial; ft./min.)	480	600	600	540	400	650
Service ceiling (ft.)	10,500	12,000	12,000	11,000	13,000	16,000
Cruising range (statute mi.)	325	460	460	340	380	238*
Fuel consumption (gal./hr.)	3.6	4.2	4.9	3.8	4.9	

*With 38 gal. optional tanks 431 mi.

Table A-3. Specifications and performance—Piper PA-11, PA-12, PA-14, and PA-18

	PA-11-65	PA-11-90	PA-12	PA-14	PA-18-90	PA-18-108	PA-18-125	PA-18-150
Engine	Cont A-65-8/9	Cont C-90	Lyc O-235	Lyc O-235-C1	Cont C-90	Lyc O-235	Lyc O-290-D	Lyc O-320-A2A
Hp and rpm	65 @ 2350	90 @ 2475	100 @ 2600	115 @ 2800	90 @ 2475	108 @ 2600	125 @ 2600	150 @ 2700
Gross weight(lbs.)	1220	1220	1750*	1850*	1300	1340	1500	1750
Empty weight (lbs.)	730	750	950	1020	840	875	845	930
Useful load (lbs.)	490	470			460	465	655	820
Wingspan (ft.)	35.25	35.25	35.5	35.5	35.3	35.3	35.3	35.4
Wing area (sq. ft.)	178.5	178.5	179.3	179.3	178.5	178.5	178.5	178.5
Length (ft.)	22.4	22.4	22.8	23.25	22.4	22.4	22.4	22.6
Height (in.)	80	80	82	77	79	79	79	80
Propeller diameter (in.)	72	72	76	74	74	74	74	74
Power loading (lbs./hp)	18.7	13.5	17.5	17.1	14.4	12.5	12	13.9
Wing loading (lbs./sq. ft.)	6.9	6.9	9.8	10.3	7.3	7.5	8.4	10
Baggage capacity (lbs.)	20	20	41	80	none	none	50	50
Fuel capacity (U.S. gal.)	18	18	38	38	18	18	18	36
Maximum speed (mph)	100	112	114	123	112	117	125	130
Cruise (mph @ 3000 ft.)	87	100	105	110	100	105	110	115
Stalling speed (mph)	38	40	42	46**	42	42	38	43
Rate of climb (initial; ft./min.)	514	900	600	600	700	850	1000	960
Service ceiling (ft.)	14,000	16,000	12,600	12,500	15,000	17,500	19,500	19,000
Absolute ceiling (ft.)	16,000	18,000	15,500	14,500	18,000	19,500		
Cruising range (statute mi.)	300	350	600	500	360	270	250	460
Fuel consumption (gal./hr.)	4.7	5	6.5	7	5	7		
Best rate of climb speed (mph)	55	55						
Takeoff run (ft.)	350	250			400	350	210**	200**

*1500 and 1550 lbs. respectively in utility category.

**With flaps.

B

Three-view drawings

The following detailed drawings of five different Cub airplanes were prepared and published by the late Paul Matt, with whom I had a long and pleasant association. Appreciation is extended to Alan Abel and Drina Welch Abel of Aviation Heritage/Sunshine House, present owners of the Matt copyrights, for their permission to reprint these internationally acclaimed drawings.

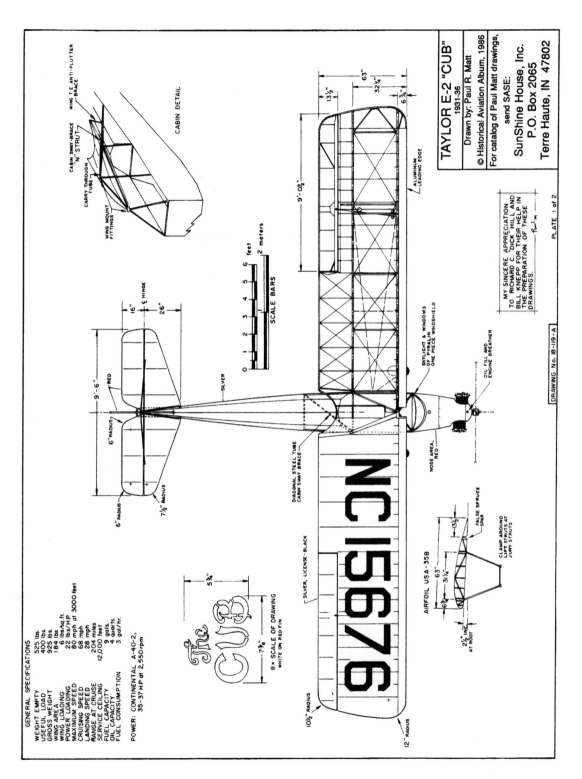

GENERAL SPECIFICATIONS

WEIGHT EMPTY   525 lbs.
USEFUL LOAD   400 lbs.
GROSS WEIGHT   925 lbs.
WING AREA   184 sq.ft.
WING LOADING   6 lbs/sq.ft.
POWER LOADING   22 lbs/HP
MAXIMUM SPEED   80 mph at 3000 feet
CRUISING SPEED   68 mph
LANDING SPEED   28 mph
RANGE AT CRUISE   204 miles
SERVICE CEILING   12,000 feet
FUEL CAPACITY   9 gals.
OIL CAPACITY   4 quarts
FUEL CONSUMPTION   3 gal/hr.

POWER: CONTINENTAL A-40-2,
35-37 HP at 2,550 rpm

The CUB
8 x SCALE OF DRAWING
WHITE ON RED FIN

TAYLOR E-2 "CUB"
1931-36
Drawn by: Paul R. Matt
© Historical Aviation Album, 1986
For catalog of Paul Matt drawings,
send SASE:
SunShine House, Inc.
P.O. Box 2065
Terre Haute, IN 47802

MY SINCERE APPRECIATION
TO RICHARD C. "DICK" HILL AND
BILL KNEPP FOR THEIR HELP IN
THE PREPARATION OF THESE
DRAWINGS.

PLATE 1 of 2

DRAWING No. 18-119-A

CABIN DETAIL

WING T.E. ANTI-FLUTTER BRACE
CABIN SWAY-BRACE "N" STRUT
CARRY THROUGH TUBE
WING MOUNT FITTINGS
ALUMINUM LEADING EDGE

SCALE BARS

SKYLIGHT & WINDOWS OF PYRALIN ONE PIECE WINDSHIELD
OIL FILL AND ENGINE BREATHER
NOSE AREA, RED
DIAGONAL STEEL TUBE CABIN SWAY BRACE

RED
SILVER
6" RADIUS
7½" RADIUS
6" RADIUS

FALSE SPRUCE SPAR
CLAMP AROUND LIFT STRUTS AT JURY STRUTS
AIRFOIL USA-35B
2½ INC. AT ROOT

SILVER, LICENSE-BLACK

10½" RADIUS
12" RADIUS

16" HINGE 26"

NC15676

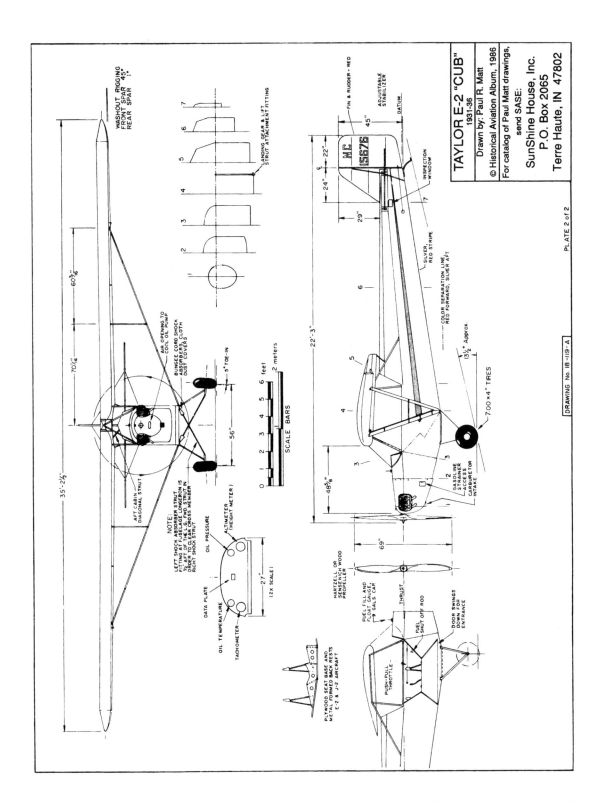

TAYLOR E-2 "CUB"
1931-36
Drawn by: Paul R. Matt
© Historical Aviation Album, 1986
For catalog of Paul Matt drawings,
send SASE:
SunShine House, Inc.
P.O. Box 2065
Terre Haute, IN 47802

DRAWING No. 18-119-A   PLATE 2 of 2

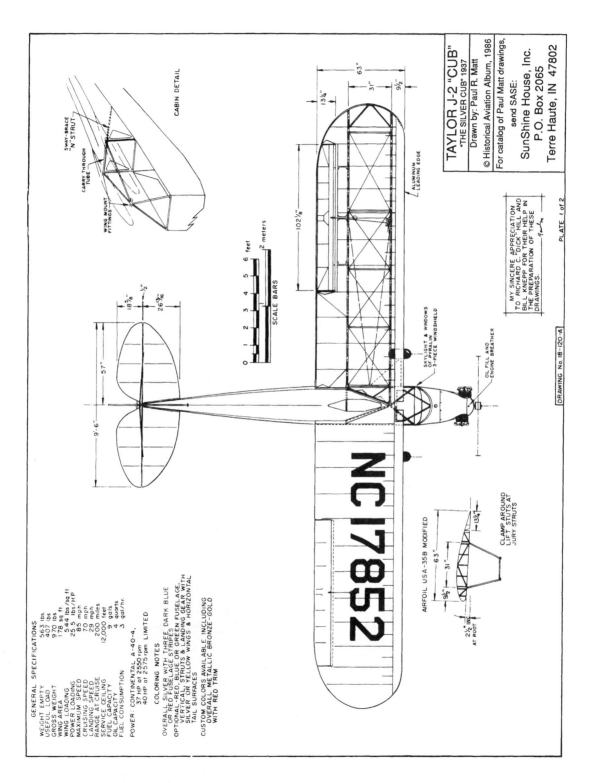

TAYLOR J-2 "CUB"
"THE SILVER CUB" 1937
Drawn by: Paul R. Matt
© Historical Aviation Album, 1986

For catalog of Paul Matt drawings,
send SASE:

SunShine House, Inc.
P.O. Box 2065
Terre Haute, IN 47802

MY SINCERE APPRECIATION
TO RICHARD C. DICK "HILL AND
BILL MNEPP FOR THEIR HELP IN
THE PREPARATION OF THESE
DRAWINGS.

PLATE 1 of 2

DRAWING No. 18-120-A

GENERAL SPECIFICATIONS

WEIGHT EMPTY   563 lbs.
USEFUL LOAD   407 lbs.
GROSS WEIGHT   970 lbs.
WING AREA   178 sq. ft.
WING LOADING   5.44 lbs./sq. ft
POWER LOADING   25.5 lbs./H.P.
MAXIMUM SPEED   85 mph
CRUISING SPEED   70 mph
LANDING SPEED   29 mph
RANGE AT CRUISE   200 miles
SERVICE CEILING   12,000 feet
FUEL CAPACITY   9 gals.
OIL CAPACITY   4 quarts
FUEL CONSUMPTION   3 gal./hr.

POWER: CONTINENTAL A-40-4,
37 HP at 2550 rpm
40 HP at 2575 rpm LIMITED

COLORING NOTES

OVERALL SILVER WITH THREE DARK BLUE
OR RED FUSELAGE STRIPES

OPTIONAL-RED, BLUE OR GREEN FUSELAGE,
VERTICAL STRUTS & LANDING GEAR WITH
SILVER OR YELLOW WINGS & HORIZONTAL
TAIL SURFACES

CUSTOM COLORS AVAILABLE INCLUDING
OVERALL METALLIC BRONZE-GOLD
WITH RED TRIM

CABIN DETAIL

SWAY-BRACE
"N" STRUT

CARRY THROUGH
TUBE

WING MOUNT
FITTINGS

SCALE BARS

feet
2 meters

ALUMINUM
LEADING EDGE

SKYLIGHT & WINDOWS
OF PYRALIN
3-PIECE WINDSHIELD

OIL FILL AND
ENGINE BREATHER

NC17852

AIRFOIL USA-35B MODIFIED

CLAMP AROUND
LIFT STRUTS AT
JURY STRUTS

2½ INC.
AT ROOT

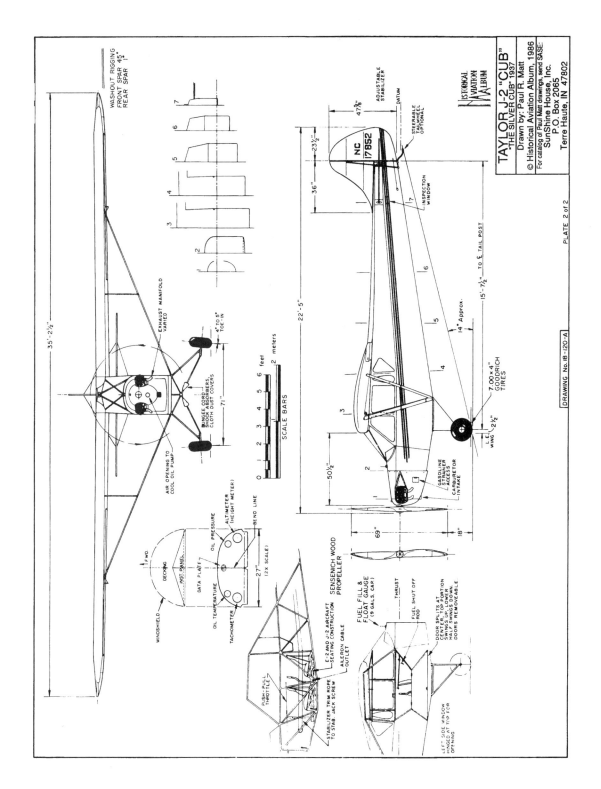

WASHOUT RIGGING
FRONT SPAR 4½°
REAR SPAR 1°

35'-2½"

EXHAUST MANIFOLD VARIED

4° TO 5" TOE-IN

71"

BUNGEE CORD, SHOCK ABSORBERS, CLOTH DUST COVERS

AIR OPENING TO COOL OIL PUMP

SCALE BARS

0 1 2 3 4 5 6 feet

0 1 2 meters

WINDSHIELD

DECKING

FWD.

INST. PANEL

DATA PLATE

OIL PRESSURE

ALTIMETER (HEIGHT METER)

BEND LINE

27"

(2X SCALE)

OIL TEMPERATURE

TACHOMETER

E-2 AND J-2 AIRCRAFT SEATING CONSTRUCTION

SENSENICH WOOD PROPELLER

AILERON CABLE OUTLET

PUSH-PULL THROTTLE

STABILIZER TRIM ROPE TO STAB. JACK SCREW

FUEL FILL & FLOAT GAUGE (9 GALS. CAP.)

THRUST

FUEL SHUT OFF ROD

DOOR SPLITS AT CENTER, TOP PORTION SWINGS UP, LOWER HALF SWINGS DOWN. DOORS REMOVEABLE.

LEFT SIDE WINDOW HINGED AT TOP FOR OPENING

ADJUSTABLE STABILIZER

DATUM

STEERABLE TAILWHEEL OPTIONAL

NC 17852

36"

23½"

47⅞"

INSPECTION WINDOW

22'-5"

14° Approx.

15'-7½" TO ₵ TAIL POST

50½"

7.00 x 4" GOODRICH TIRES

2½"

L.E. WING

GASOLINE STRAINER ACCESS

CARBURETOR INTAKE

69"

18"

TAYLOR J-2 "CUB"
"THE SILVER CUB" 1937

Drawn by: Paul R. Matt

© Historical Aviation Album, 1986

For catalog of Paul Matt drawings, send SASE:
SunShine House, Inc.
P.O. Box 2065
Terre Haute, IN 47802

Historical Aviation Album

PLATE 2 of 2

DRAWING No. 18-120-A

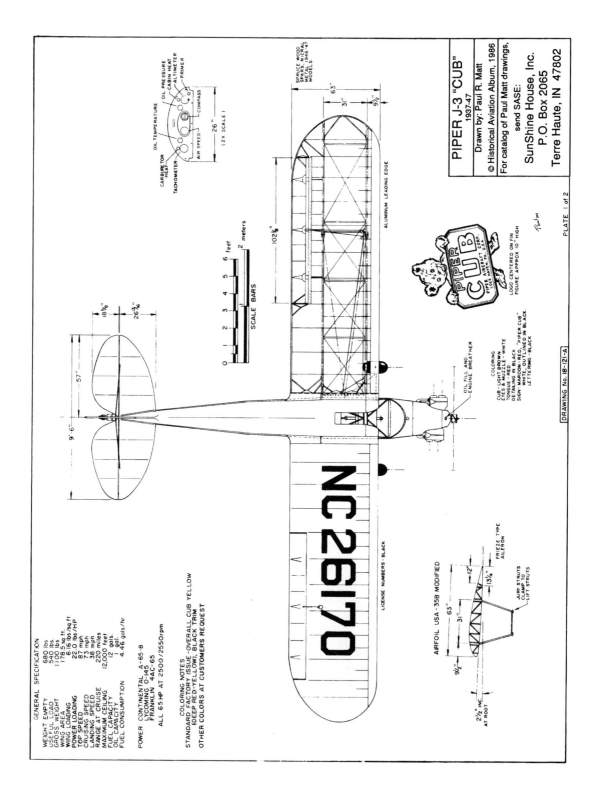

GENERAL SPECIFICATION

WEIGHT EMPTY   680 lbs
USEFUL LOAD   540 lbs.
GROSS WEIGHT   1100 lbs.
WING AREA   175.5 sq.ft.
WING LOADING   6.6 lbs/sq.ft.
POWER LOADING   22.0 lbs/HP
TOP SPEED   87 mph
CRUISING SPEED   73 mph
LANDING SPEED   38 mph
RANGE AT CRUISE   220 miles
MAXIMUM CEILING   12,000 feet
FUEL CAPACITY   12 gals.
OIL CAPACITY   1 gal.
FUEL CONSUMPTION   4.46 gals/hr

POWER CONTINENTAL A-65-8
       LYCOMING O-145
       FRANKLIN 4AC-65

       ALL 65 HP AT 2500/2550rpm

COLORING NOTES
STANDARD FACTORY ISSUE-OVERALL CUB YELLOW
(DEEP RED-YELLOW), BLACK TRIM
OTHER COLORS AT CUSTOMERS REQUEST

OIL TEMPERATURE
OIL PRESSURE
CABIN HEAT
ALTIMETER
PRIMER
COMPASS
(2X SCALE)
26"
AIR SPEED
TACHOMETER
CARBURETOR HEAT

18⅝"   26⅛"

57"

9'-6"

ALUMINUM LEADING EDGE

SPRUCE WOOD,
SPARS IN METAL,
METAL IN METAL
MODELS 1946-47

63"
31"   9½"

102⅝"

OIL FILL AND
ENGINE BREATHER

LICENSE NUMBERS - BLACK

NC26170

SCALE BARS

0 1 2 3 4 5 6 feet
            2 meters

COLORING
CUB-LIGHT BROWN
EYES & MUZZLE-WHITE
TONGUE-RED
DETAILING IN BLACK
SIGN-MAROON-RED, "PIPER CUB"
WHITE, OUTLINED IN BLACK
LETTERING -BLACK

LOGO CENTERED ON FIN
FIGURE APPROX 10" HIGH

AIRFOIL USA -35B MODIFIED

63"
31"
9½"

13¼"
12"

FRIEZE TYPE
AILERON

JURY STRUTS
CLAMP TO
LIFT STRUTS

2½" INC.
AT ROOT

PIPER J-3 "CUB"
1937-47
Drawn by: Paul R. Matt
© Historical Aviation Album, 1986
For catalog of Paul Matt drawings,
send SASE:
SunShine House, Inc.
P.O. Box 2065
Terre Haute, IN 47802

PLATE 1 of 2

DRAWING No. IB-121-A

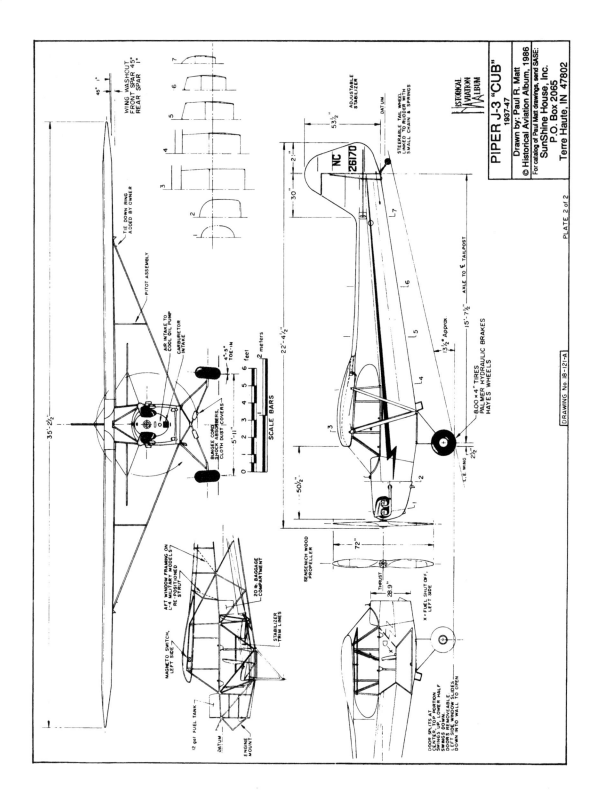

WING WASHOUT
FRONT SPAR 45°
REAR SPAR 1°

TIE DOWN RING
ADDED BY OWNER

PITOT ASSEMBLY

AIR INTAKE TO
COOL OIL PUMP

CARBURETOR
INTAKE

BUNGEE CORD
SHOCK ABSORBERS,
CLOTH DUST COVERS

4°-5°
TOE-IN

5'-11"

35'-2½"

SCALE BARS

2 meters

6 feet

ADJUSTABLE
STABILIZER

DATUM

STEERABLE TAIL WHEEL,
LINKED TO RUDDER WITH
SMALL CHAIN & SPRINGS

NC
26170

53½'

30"

2"

22'-4½"

50½"

8.00 × 4" TIRES
PALMER HYDRAULIC BRAKES
HAYES WHEELS

13½' Approx.

15'-7½"

AXLE TO ₵ TAILPOST

L.E. WING

2½'

AFT WINDOW FRAMING ON
L-4 MILITARY MODELS
RE-POSITIONED

STRUT

20 lb. BAGGAGE
COMPARTMENT

MAGNETO SWITCH,
LEFT SIDE

STABILIZER
TRIM LINES

12 gal FUEL TANK

DATUM

ENGINE
MOUNT

SENSENICH WOOD
PROPELLER

72"

THRUST

28.9"

X = FUEL SHUT OFF,
LEFT SIDE

DOOR SPLITS AT
CENTER, TOP PORTION
SWINGS UP, LOWER HALF
SWINGS DOWN.
DOORS REMOVEABLE.
LEFT SIDE WINDOW SLIDES
DOWN INTO WALL TO OPEN

PIPER J-3 "CUB"
1937-47

Drawn by: Paul R. Matt
© Historical Aviation Album, 1986

For catalog of Paul Matt drawings, send SASE:
SunShine House, Inc.
P.O. Box 2065
Terre Haute, IN 47802

HISTORICAL
AVIATION
ALBUM

PLATE 2 of 2

DRAWING No.18-121-A

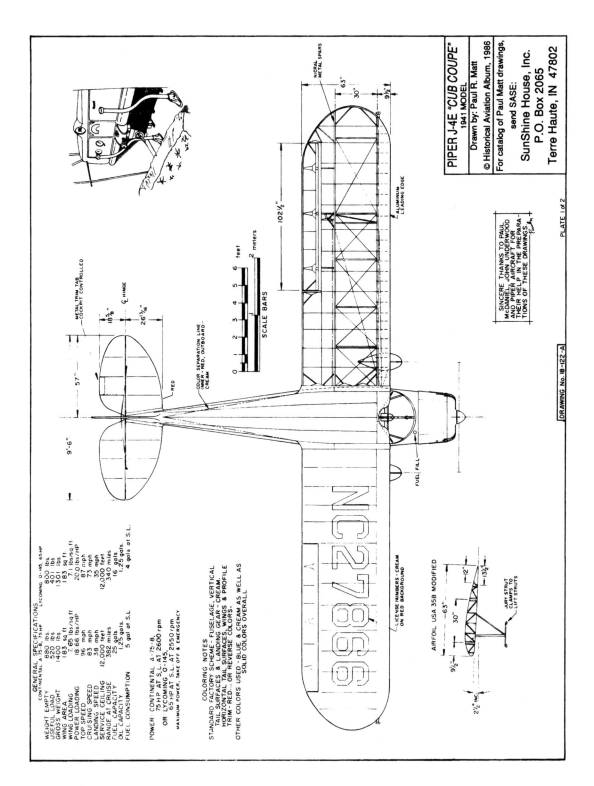

PIPER J-4E "CUB COUPE"
1941 MODEL

Drawn by: Paul R. Matt

© Historical Aviation Album, 1986

For catalog of Paul Matt drawings,
send SASE:

SunShine House, Inc.
P.O. Box 2065
Terre Haute, IN 47802

SINCERE THANKS TO PAUL McDANIEL, JOHN UNDERWOOD AND PIPER AIRCRAFT FOR THEIR HELP IN THE PREPARATIONS OF THESE DRAWINGS.

PLATE 1 of 2

DRAWING No. 18-122-A

NICRAL METAL SPARS

ALUMINUM LEADING EDGE

63"
30"
9½"
102½"

METAL TRIM TAB
COCKPIT CONTROLLED

18⅝"

26¹³⁄₁₆"

Ç HINGE

57"

RED

COLOR SEPARATION LINE
INNER - RED, OUTBOARD -
CREAM

9'-6"

SCALE BARS

0 1 2 3 4 5 6 feet
      1 2 meters

NC27866

FUEL FILL

LICENSE NUMBERS - CREAM
ON RED BACKGROUND

AIRFOIL USA 35B MODIFIED

63"
30"
9½"
12"
13½"
2½" INC.

JURY STRUT
CLAMPS TO
LIFT STRUTS

GENERAL SPECIFICATIONS
CONTINENTAL A-75-8, 75 HP   LYCOMING O-145, 65 HP
WEIGHT EMPTY   880 lbs.   800 lbs.
USEFUL LOAD   520 lbs.   401 lbs.
GROSS WEIGHT   1400 lbs.   1301 lbs.
WING AREA   183 sq. ft.
WING LOADING   7.65 lbs/sq.ft.
POWER LOADING   18.66 lbs/HP   20.0 lbs/HP
TOP SPEED   96 mph   87 mph
CRUISING SPEED   83 mph   73 mph
LANDING SPEED   38 mph   35 mph
SERVICE CEILING   12,000 feet   12,000 feet
RANGE AT CRUISE   382 miles   340 miles
FUEL CAPACITY   25 gals.   16 gals.
OIL CAPACITY   1.25 gals.   1.25 gals.
FUEL CONSUMPTION   5 gal at S.L.   4 gals at S.L.

POWER: CONTINENTAL A-75-8,
       75 HP AT S.L. AT 2600 rpm
   OR LYCOMING O-145,
       65 HP AT S.L. AT 2550 rpm
       MAXIMUM POWER, TAKE OFF & EMERGENCY

COLORING NOTES
STANDARD FACTORY SCHEME: FUSELAGE, VERTICAL
TAIL SURFACES & LANDING GEAR - CREAM.
HORIZONTAL TAIL SURFACES, WINGS & PROFILE
TRIM - RED... OR REVERSE COLORS.

OTHER COLORS USED - BLUE & CREAM AS WELL AS
SOLID COLORS OVERALL.

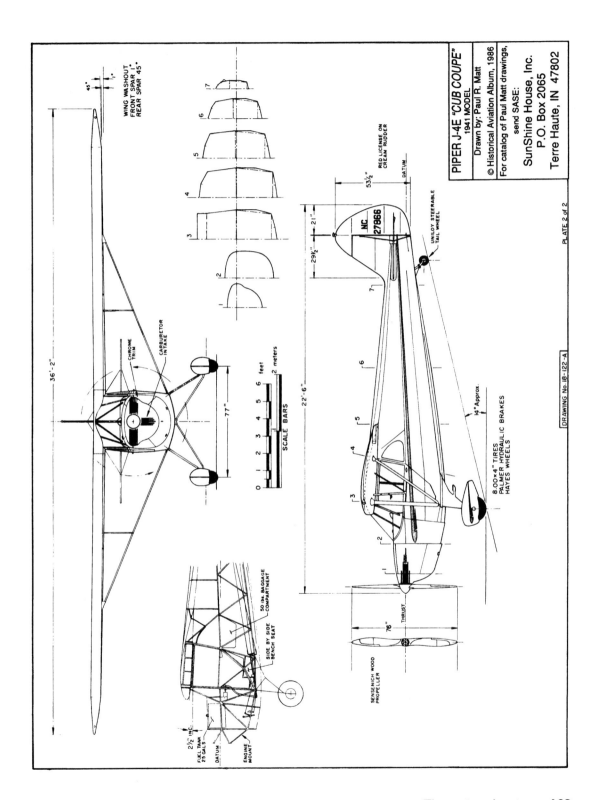

WING WASHOUT
FRONT SPAR 1°
REAR SPAR 45°

PIPER J-4E "CUB COUPE"
1941 MODEL
Drawn by: Paul R. Matt
© Historical Aviation Album, 1986
For catalog of Paul Matt drawings,
send SASE:
SunShine House, Inc.
P.O. Box 2065
Terre Haute, IN 47802

RED LICENSE ON
CREAM RUDDER

DATUM

NC
27866

UNILOY STEERABLE
TAIL WHEEL

14° Approx.

8.00×4" TIRES
PALMER HYDRAULIC BRAKES
HAYES WHEELS

PLATE 2 of 2

DRAWING No. 18-122-A

53½"

21"

29½"

22'-6"

CHROME
TRIM

CARBURETOR
INTAKE

36'-2"

77"

SCALE BARS

0   1   2   3   4   5   6   feet
        2 meters

THRUST

76"

SENSENICH WOOD
PROPELLER

50 lbs. BAGGAGE
COMPARTMENT

SIDE BY SIDE
BENCH SEAT

FUEL TANK
25 GALS.

DATUM

ENGINE
MOUNT

2½" INC.

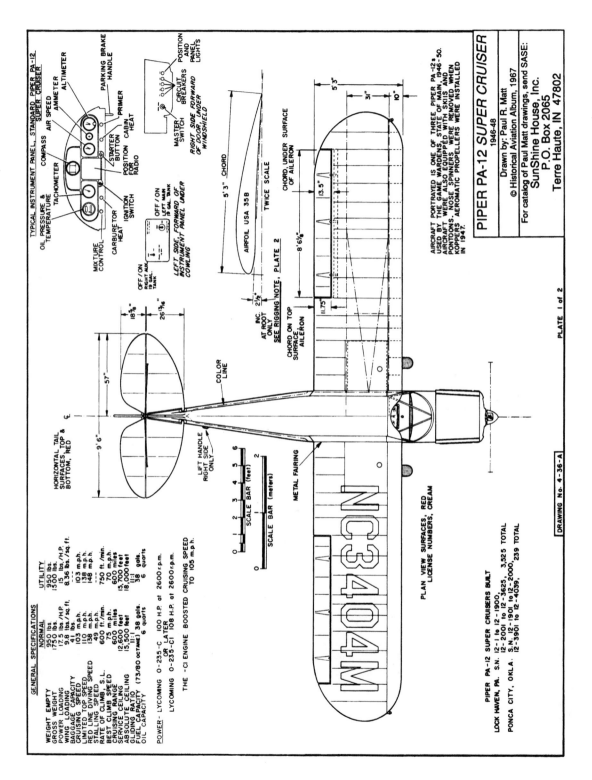

TYPICAL INSTRUMENT PANEL, STANDARD PIPER PA-12
SUPER CRUISER

PARKING BRAKE HANDLE
ALTIMETER
AIR SPEED
AMMETER
COMPASS
OIL PRESSURE & TEMPERATURE
TACHOMETER
MIXTURE CONTROL
CARBURETOR HEAT
IGNITION SWITCH
POSITION FOR RADIO
PRIMER
CABIN HEAT
STARTER BUTTON

MASTER SWITCH
CIRCUIT BREAKERS
POSITION AND PANEL LIGHTS
RIGHT SIDE FORWARD OF DOOR, UNDER WINDSHIELD

OFF / ON
LEFT MAIN 19 GAL. TANK
OFF / ON
RIGHT AUX. 19 GAL. TANK

LEFT SIDE, FORWARD OF INSTRUMENT PANEL UNDER COWLING

GENERAL SPECIFICATIONS

	NORMAL	UTILITY
WEIGHT EMPTY	950 lbs.	950 lbs.
GROSS WEIGHT	1750 lbs.	1500 lbs.
POWER LOADING	17.5 lbs./H.P.	15 lbs./H.P.
WING LOADING	9.8 lbs./sq.ft.	8.36 lbs./sq.ft.
BAGGAGE CAPACITY	41 lbs.	
CRUISING SPEED	103 m.p.h.	103 m.p.h.
LIMITED TOP SPEED	110 m.p.h.	138 m.p.h.
RED LINE DIVING SPEED	138 m.p.h.	148 m.p.h.
STALLING SPEED	49 m.p.h.	
RATE OF CLIMB S.L.	600 ft./min.	750 ft./min.
BEST CLIMB SPEED	75 m.p.h.	70 m.p.h.
CRUISING RANGE	600 miles	600 miles
SERVICE CEILING	12,600 feet	15,700 feet
ABSOLUTE CEILING	15,500 feet	18,000 feet
GLIDING RATIO	11:1	11:1
FUEL CAPACITY (73/80 octane)	38 gals.	38 gals.
OIL CAPACITY	6 quarts	6 quarts

POWER— LYCOMING 0-235-C 100 H.P. at 2600 r.p.m.

LYCOMING 0-235-C1 108 H.P. at 2600 r.p.m.

THE -C1 ENGINE BOOSTED CRUISING SPEED TO 105 m.p.h.

COLOR LINE

HORIZONTAL TAIL SURFACES, TOP & BOTTOM, RED

18⅛"
26¹³/₁₆"
57"
9'6"

LIFT HANDLE RIGHT SIDE ONLY

METAL FAIRING

NC3404M

SCALE BAR (feet)
SCALE BAR (meters)

PLAN VIEW SURFACES, RED
LICENSE NUMBERS, CREAM

PIPER PA-12 SUPER CRUISERS BUILT
LOCK HAVEN, PA. S.N. 12-1 to 12-1900,   12-2001 to 12-3625, 3,525 TOTAL
PONCA CITY, OKLA. S.N. 12-1901 to 12-2000, 239 TOTAL
12-3901 to 12-4039,

5' 3"
5'3" CHORD
AIRFOIL USA 35 B
TWICE SCALE
2½"
INC. AT ROOT ONLY
SEE RIGGING NOTE, PLATE 2

CHORD ON TOP SURFACE, AILERON

CHORD, UNDER SURFACE OF AILERON
13.5"
8'6½"
11.75"

5' 3"
3"
10"

AIRCRAFT PORTRAYED IS ONE OF THREE PIPER PA-12's USED BY THE GAME WARDENS, STATE OF MAIN, 1946-50. AIRCRAFT WERE ALSO EQUIPPED WITH SKIS AND PONTOONS. NOSE SPINNERS WERE REMOVED WHEN KOPPERS AEROMATIC PROPELLERS WERE INSTALLED IN 1947.

PIPER PA-12 SUPER CRUISER
1946-48

Drawn by: Paul R. Matt
© Historical Aviation Album, 1967
For catalog of Paul Matt drawings, send SASE:
SunShine House, Inc.
P.O. Box 2065
Terre Haute, IN 47802

PLATE 1 of 2

DRAWING No. 4-36-A

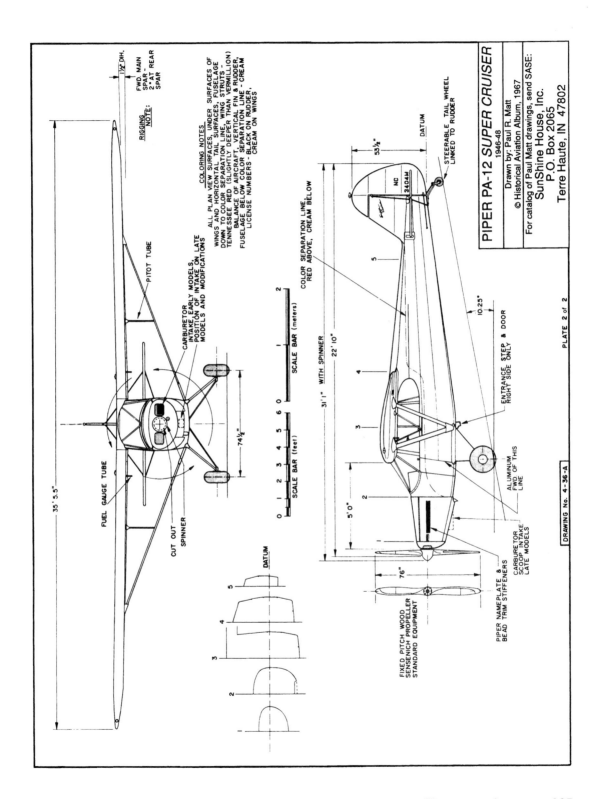

C

Military
serial numbers

The military serial number on an airplane is often the only way that historians and other interested parties can distinguish between such outwardly identical airplanes as Piper L-4As and L-4Hs.

This appendix has been compiled to assist you in identifying military Cubs from photographs. The numbers listed are all in sequential order, making it a simple matter to match any serial number appearing on a photo to its number in the left-hand column of the table and the corresponding model number in the "Model" column.

U.S. Army Cub serial numbers

Since January 1942, the serial number of U.S. Army airplanes has appeared on both sides of the vertical tail, and is generally referred to as the "tail number." The number consists of two parts—the fiscal year in which the airplane was ordered and its sequence of procurement within that year. The serial number 42-460 on the first Piper YO-59 means that it was the 460th U.S. Army airplane ordered in the Government's fiscal year 1942 (July 1, 1941 through June 30, 1942).

However, the number does not appear on the tail this way. The first digit of the year figure is deleted, as is the dash, so 42–460 appears only as 2460. Unfortunately for those trying to identify various L-4 variants from photographs, Piper was not consistent in applying the tail numbers. However, in such cases, and when camera angles and lighting permit, the full serial number, as well as the airplane designation, can be read in the Technical Data Legend that appears below the windshield on the left side of the airplane. See L-4K in Fig. 5-21 on page 64.

U.S. Army serial numbers	U.S. Army model	Quantity
42-640/463	YO-59	4
42-7813/7952	O-59	140
42-15159/15329	O-59A	171
42-36325/36824	O-59A	500
42-38380/38457	L-4A	178
42-57507	L-4F	1
42-79551/79554	L-4F	4
42-79555	UC-83B/L-4E	1
42-79557, 79558	UC-83A/L-4C	2
42-107425	L-4F	1
43-491/1470	L-4B	980
43-2909	L-4F	1
43-2910	L-4G	1
43-2911, 2912	L-4F	2
43-2913	L-4G	1
43-2914	L-4D	1
43-2915/2920	L-4F	6
43-2921	L-4G	1
43-2922	L-4F	1
43-2923	L-4C	1
43-2924	L-4D	1
43-2925	L-4C	1
43-2926	L-4F	1
43-2927	L-4C	1
43-2928, 2929	L-4G	2
43-2930, 2931	L-4F	2
43-2932	L-4C	1
43-2933	L-4G	1
43-2934, 2935	L-4F	2
43-2936	L-4G	1
43-2937/2939	L-4F	3
43-2940	L-4G	1
43-2941	L-4E	1
43-2942/2946	L-4G	5
43-2947	L-4F	1
43-2948	L-4G	1
43-2949	L-4F	1
43-2950, 2951	L-4G	2
43-2952, 2953	L-4F	2
43-2954/2958	L-4E	5
43-2959	L-4C	1

U.S. Army serial numbers	U.S. Army model	Quantity
43-2963	L-4G	1
43-2964/2966	L-4F	3
43-2967	L-4C	1
43-2968/2970	L-4F	3
43-2971, 2972	L-4G	2
43-2973, 2974	L-4E	2
43-2975/2977	L-4G	3
43-2978	L-4F	1
43-2979	L-4G	1
43-2980	L-4F	1
43-2981/2988	L-4G	8
43-2989, 2990	L-4E	2
43-2991	L-4F	1
43-2992	L-4D	1
43-2994	L-4G	1
43-2995, 2996	L-4D	2
43-2997, 2998	L-4G	2
43-2999/3002	L-4F	4
43-3003/3008	L-4E	6
43-3009/3258	TG-8	50
43-12499/12501	TG-8	3
43-29247/3054	L-4H	1301
44-52988	L-4F	1
44-79545/80044	L-4H	500
44-80045/80844	L-4J	800
45-4401/5200	L-4J	800
45-55175/55215	L-4J	141
45-55255/55257	L-4J	3
45-55259, 55260	L-4J	2
45-55263, 55264	L-4J	2
49-2774/2878	L-18B	105
50-1745/1812	L-18C	68
51-6495, 6496	YL-21	2
51-15272, 15329	L-18C	58
51-15330/15653	L-18C	324
51-15654/15803	L-21A	150
51-16086/16091	J-5A*	6
52-2376/2539	L-18C	164
52-6220/6294	L-21B	75
53-3738/3784	L-21B	47**
53-4665/4848	L-18C	184

U.S. Army serial numbers	U.S. Army model	Quantity
53-4849/4877	L-21B	29
53-7718/7779	L-21B	62***
54-719/758	L-18C	40
54-2309/2663	L-21B	355
54-2826/2835	L-21B	10
55-4578/4581	L-21B	4
55-4749	L-18C	1
61-2928, 2929	L-21B	2

*Civil acquisition for MDAP

**All to Japan.

***All to Italy.

U.S. Navy Cub serial numbers

All of the U.S. Navy's WWII Cubs carried serial numbers in a third series that started at 0001 in 1941. This number, called the BuNo because it was issued by the Bureau of Aeronautics, appeared on either side of the vertical fin of U.S. Navy planes from 1925 until after WWII in three-inch block figures. The model designation, NE-1, AE-1, etc., appeared in line with the BuNo, but on the rudder.

U.S. Navy BuNo	U.S. Navy model	Quantity
26196/26425	NE-1	230
29669/29688	NE-2	20*
30197/30296	HE-1/AE-1	100
36425/36427**	XLNP-1	3

*Last 10 not delivered

**Ex-U.S. Army TG-8 43-3065, 3070, 3075

Royal Air Force Cub serial numbers

Britain's Royal Air Force operated a total of 26 Cubs, all but five of them drafted from private owners. The others were U.S. Army L-4Bs obtained under Lend-Lease.

RAF serial number	Piper model	Registration	C/N
BT440	J-4A	G-AFSZ	4-538
BT441	J-4A	G-AFVL	4-543
BT442	J-4A	G-AFWR	4-589
BV180	J-4A	G-AFWA	4-558
BV181	J-4A	G-AFWB	4-559

RAF serial number	Piper model	Registration	C/N
BV984	J-4A	NC24731	——
BV985	J-4A	NC24761	——
BV986	J-4A	NC24741	4-707
BV987	J-4A	G-AFVG	4-588
BV988	J-4A	G-AFVM	4-554
BV989	J-4A	G-AFTB	4-541
BV990	J-4B	G-AFTC	4-525
BV991	J-4A	G-AFVF	4-586
DG667	J-4A	G-AFXS	4-647
DP582	J-4A	G-AFXT	4-653
ES923	J-4A	G-AFWS	4-613
HL530	J-4A	EI-ABZ*	——
HL531	J-4A	G-AFTD	4-542
HM565	J-4A	G-AFSY	4-510
——	J-4A	G-AFWV	4-622
——	J-4A	G-AFWW	4-618
——	J-3C**	G-AFIY	2425
FR886/889	L-4B	See page 59	
VM286	L-4B		

*From Ireland

**Tested but rejected

D

Cub deliveries
1931–1992

Because 61 years of production cannot be presented in a single table, Cub production from 1931 to May 1992 is presented in a series of four slightly differing tables. It should be noted that several different "official" sources differ slightly on the totals of each Cub model. The totals presented in these tables and throughout this book are the most accurate, in my belief.

Table D-1. Civil Cub Deliveries (1931–1941)

Year	E-2	J-2	J-3	J-4	J-5
1931	22				
1932	22				
1933	17				
1934	71*				
1935	212				
1936	7	515			
1937		658	25		
1938		23	647	31	
1939			1347	403	
1940			1977	540	488
1941			1855	250	776
Total built	351	1196	See Table D-2 for totals		

* Includes all F-2

203

Table D-2. Civil Cub Deliveries (1942–1952)
(See Table D-3 for PA-18 Super Cub)

Year	J-3	J-4	J-5	L-14	PA-11	PA-12	PA-14
1942	296*	26	140				
1943							
1944	No civil production (1943 and 1944)						
1945	938			9**			
1946	6320					1453	
1947	720				614	2158	
1948					578	146	192
1949					233	1	38
1950					3		1
1951							
1952							1
Total built	14,125	1250	1404	9	1428	3758	232

* 230 taken by Navy as NE-1

** Military model delivered as civil

Table D-3. Civil PA-18 Super Cub Deliveries (1949–1992)

Year	PA-18	PA-18A	Year	PA-18
1949	20		1971	57
1950	454		1972	29
1951	480		1973	20
1952	248	229	1974	146
1953	242	258	1975	138
1954	185	213	1976	178
1955	244	361	1977	201
1956	311	416	1978	178
1957	300	499	1979	182
1958	181	343	1980	52
1959	190	280	1981	69
1960	278	51	1982	54
1961	199		1983	None built
1962	141		1984	(1983–1987)
1963	188		1985	
1964	119		1986	

Year	PA-18	PA-18A		Year	PA-18
1965	145			1987	
1966	138			1988	2
1967	140			1989	49
1968	138			1990	6
1969	90			1991	0
1970	57			1992	1

Total built 8501

Table D-4. Military Cub Deliveries (1941–1958)

Year	O-59/L-4	NE-1	HE-1	TG-8	L-14	L-18	L-21	PA-18T [5]
1941	4							
1942	1711	230[1]	20					
1943	1102		80	100				
1944	2001			153				
1945	859				5[2]			
1946								
1947		No military deliveries in 1946, 1947, or 1948						
1948								
1949						105[3]		
1950						68[4]		
1951							122	
1952						799	16	27
1953							135	216
1954							298	
1955						1	66	
1956							67	
1957							11	
1958							1	
Total built	5677	230	100	253	5	973	716	243

[1] From 1942 civil production

[2] 9 others as civil

[3] PA-11/L-18B

[4] PA-18/L-18C from here on

[5] Delivered with civil registrations

Index